THE LITERARY 1920s

"...and say my glory was I had such friends." —W.B. Yeats

KATHLEEN DIXON DONNELLY

"Such Friends": The Literary 1920s, Vol. 1—1920
©2021 by Kathleen Dixon Donnelly

Published by K. Donnelly Communications, Pittsburgh, PA, USA
Printed in the United States of America

ISBN (paperback): 978-1-7364831-0-7

ISBN (eBook): 978-1-7364831-1-4

Other books by Kathleen Dixon Donnelly, available on Amazon

Manager as Muse: Maxwell Perkins' Work with F. Scott Fitzgerald, Ernest Hemingway and Thomas Wolfe

Gypsy Teacher, a book of blogs chronicling the author's voyages sailing on Semester at Sea and relocating to the United Kingdom

Cover and interior designed by Lisa Thomson, LisaT2@comcast.net

Cover photo by Kathleen Dixon Donnelly is of The Autograph Tree at Lady Augusta Gregory's home, Coole Park in the west of Ireland. Lady Gregory had her guests carve their names and initials into the trunk of the tree.

To Tony, Willie and Gussie

My best "such friends"

*"Think where man's glory most begins and ends,
and say my glory was I had such friends."*

*—The Municipal Gallery Revisited,
William Butler Yeats*

PREFACE

In the early years of the 20th century, it was common for writers and artists on both sides of the Atlantic to gather in living rooms, drawing rooms, pubs and cafes—salons—to discuss the latest happenings in the arts, read to each other from their latest works, and gossip.

In the English-speaking Western world, there were four main groups—

- **William Butler Yeats** and the Irish Literary Renaissance,
- **Virginia Woolf** and the Bloomsbury Group,
- **Gertrude Stein** and the Americans in Paris, and
- **Dorothy Parker** and the Algonquin Round Table.

The Irish and English met together in their groups before the "Great War" (1914-1918), but remained friends and active in their creative fields well into the 1920s. The Americans in Paris and New York were most active right after the Armistice and throughout the next decade.

They worked on projects—the Abbey Theater for the Irish, the Omega Workshops for some of the Bloomsberries—but mostly they hung out. They had places in the city and places in the country that they decorated and made their own.

The burst of creativity that became modernism was brought about by men and women of extraordinary talent and ordinary pursuits. They ate, they drank, they neglected their families. They praised and berated each other privately and publicly; they bickered endlessly. They complained about money and few had day jobs. And they talked. And talked.

My Ph.D. in Communications from Dublin City University in Ireland focused on the relationships among the creative people in these four salons. Since then I have expanded my research to include many artists, writers and supporters of the arts who orbited around the original key players. A discussion of the literary life of the early 20th century is not complete without T. S. Eliot, James Joyce, Edna St. Vincent Millay, and Thomas Wolfe for example, although none was really a part of any salon.

I have posted blogs [www.suchfriends.wordpress.com], led walking tours, self-published a book and given presentations about all these creative people under the title "Such Friends," taken from **Yeats'** line, "…and say my glory was I had such friends."

As the year 2020 approached, I realized there were going to be a whole lot of centenary celebrations in the coming decade: Prohibition goes into effect (1920). The first novels of **F. Scott Fitzgerald** (*This Side of Paradise*, 1920), and **Ernest Hemingway** (*The Sun Also Rises*, 1926), are published. *Ulysses* and *The Waste Land* are both published in the same year (1922). *Mrs. Dalloway, The Great Gatsby* and *The New Yorker* magazine appear in the same year (1925). And then, just as both *A Farewell to Arms* and *Look Homeward, Angel* are published by Scribner's (October, 1929), the decade ends with a crash.

So I began to chronicle the events of 100 years ago in my blog, with the idea of pulling them together in a book. This book. And, hopefully, nine more which will follow, each one describing what was going on in the literary life of another year.

The list of the writers and artists I included in each group in my original research is on the next two pages, and their names appear in boldface throughout the book.

You can dip in and out of the vignettes in *"Such Friends": The Literary 1920s, Vol. 1—1920*, search to see if your birthday is included, look for mentions of your favorite writers, or read it all straight through from January 1st to December 31st.

Come with me back to a year when a pandemic had ended, Prohibition had started, a presidential election campaign rolled out, and these writers and artists were re-inventing their creative fields. This is a perfect opportunity to spend some time with "Such Friends."

Complete List of "Such Friends"

The Irish Literary Renaissance (1897-1906)

William Butler Yeats, poet, playwright
Lady Augusta Gregory, playwright
George Moore, novelist, playwright
AE (George Russell), artist, poet, playwright
Edward Martyn, playwright, philanthropist
John Millington Synge, playwright
Douglas Hyde, playwright, translator, politician

The Bloomsbury Group (1907-1915)

Virginia Woolf, novelist, essayist
Vanessa Bell, painter, illustrator
Lytton Strachey, essayist, biographer, critic
Duncan Grant, painter
Leonard Woolf, editor, critic, publisher, political writer
Clive Bell, art critic, essayist
Roger Fry, art critic, painter
John Maynard Keynes, economist, essayist

The Americans in Paris (1921-1930)

Gertrude Stein, novelist, essayist, librettist
Alice B. Toklas, cook, publisher, writer
Ernest Hemingway, short story writer, novelist
F. Scott Fitzgerald, novelist, short story writer
Robert McAlmon, poet, novelist, publisher
Virgil Thomson, music critic, composer
Sherwood Anderson, novelist, short story writer
Man Ray, photographer, painter

The Algonquin Round Table (1919-1928)

Dorothy Parker, essayist, short story writer, poet, critic
Robert Benchley, humorist, critic, actor
Alexander Woollcott, critic, broadcaster, actor
Marc Connelly, playwright, actor
Harold Ross, reporter, editor
George S Kaufman, playwright, director
FPA (Franklin P. Adams), columnist, critic, broadcaster
Heywood Broun, columnist, sports writer, union organizer

ACKNOWLEDGEMENTS

Where to begin?! My own "such friends" have been so supportive ever since I first moved to Dublin to work on my Ph.D.

Particular thanks go to my husband, partner, Steeler buddy, and my favorite Irishman, Tony Dixon. [And also to Willie Yeats and his late sister Lady Augusta Gregory.]

Pulling all this together in the middle of a pandemic had its challenges. And I couldn't have met and overcome them without the help of Liz and Kevin Tafel-Hurley's keen eye and reliable printer.

To double check wording, places and dates I sometimes relied on professionals who would know best. So a special thank you to Linda Tashbook for her input on posts about legal issues; Peter Monteith, Assistant Archivist at King's College, Cambridge; Richard Webb at Gatsby in Connecticut [https://gatsbyinct.com/]; and those at the Ogunquit Library and the Historical Society of Wells and Ogunquit, in Maine.

Decades ago I was able to publish all by myself on Lulu, but those days are gone. This book would not have happened without the work of Lisa Thomson, designer, and Loral Pepoon, co-owner of Selah Press Publishing, who saved me countless hours of frustration.

Fortunately, early on I decided to not post anything unless someone else had read it. First Reader Tony soon got tired of this role, so I spread it out among my many friends in many countries. Thanks to all of you for your help!

Julian Asenjo
Staci Backauskas
Melanie Bond
Clarence Curry
Jim Doan
Erin C. Donnelly
Patrick J. Donnelly
Helen Fallon
Gregg Grefenstette
Marie Hooper
David Hope
Kevin Hurley
Mary Lou Irish
Nicola Jones
Maura Judges
Hedda Kopf

Howard Manns
Alyce Marshall
Philomena Mason
Maureen McKenna
Emily Midorikawa
Anton Perreau
Janet Purtell
Scott Rossi
Susan Snyder Sponar
Emma Claire Sweeney
Liz Tafel-Hurley
Linda Tashbook
Eva Tumiel-Kozak
Gaby Walter
Neil Weatherall
Mary Wiemann

✖ JANUARY 1, 1920 ✖

❝ America was going on the greatest, gaudiest spree in history and there was going to be plenty to tell about it."

—F. Scott Fitzgerald

That was 100 years ago. So here we are again. At the beginning of the Twenties. Will this be a similar decade?

There's one way to tell: To look back at certain points and document what was happening a century before, with the artists and writers who were "Such Friends":

> **William Butler Yeats** and the Irish Literary Renaissance,
> **Virginia Woolf** and the Bloomsbury Group,
> **Gertrude Stein** and the Americans in Paris, and
> **Dorothy Parker** and the Algonquin Round Table,

As the new decade begins…

In Ireland, poet **W. B. Yeats,** 54, is getting ready to go back to the United States on his third American lecture tour, this time with his wife, Georgie, 28. They are leaving the baby Anne, just 11 months old, with his sisters.

Georgie and William Butler Yeats

Virginia and Leonard Woolf

In England, Hogarth Press owners, novelist **Virginia Woolf**, about to turn 38, and her husband **Leonard**, 39, have been celebrating the holidays at Monk's House in East Sussex, which they bought last year at auction. This coming year, they want to spend more time outside of too-busy London.

In Paris, American writer **Gertrude Stein**, 45, and her partner, **Alice B. Toklas**, 42, are still working on getting back to normal after the Armistice. Their apartment, on the Left Bank near the Luxembourg Gardens, had hosted salons for all the local painters before the Great War. Who will come now?

In New York City, *Vanity Fair* writers **Dorothy Parker**, 26, **Robert Benchley**, 30, and their "such friends" have been lunching regularly at the Algonquin Hotel in midtown since last summer when everyone came back from the war. Now they

Alice B. Toklas and Gertrude Stein

Dorothy Parker

are trying to drink up in the last few weeks before the Volstead Act—Prohibition—goes into effect. They're not going to let that slow them down.

Join me on a journey through *The Literary 1920s*, tracking these characters in their place and time, 100 years ago. Happy New Year!

❧ JANUARY **10, 1920** ❧
NEW ORLEANS, LOUISIANA

F Scott Fitzgerald, 23, is eagerly anticipating receiving the galleys for his first novel, *This Side of Paradise*, so he can correct them during his self-imposed writing retreat here in New Orleans. He is writing to his editor, Maxwell Perkins, 35, at Charles Scribner's Sons in Manhattan, about his next novel:

> " I want to start it, but I don't want to get broke in the middle and… have to write short stories again—because I don't enjoy [writing stories] and just do it for money…There's nothing in collections of short stories is there?"

A week later, Perkins writes back confirming **Fitzgerald's** suspicions, but offering some encouragement:

> " It seems to me that [your stories] have the popular note which would be likely to make them sell in book form. I wish you did care more about writing them… because they have great value in making you a reputation and because they are quite worthwhile in themselves…Still we should not like to interfere with your novels…"

Max Perkins

Perkins believes it's a good idea to follow an author's novel with a short story collection, increasing sales of both.

✺ JANUARY **16, 1920** ✺
AMERICA

All across the country, in bars and saloons—and churches—people are waiting for the stroke of midnight. When America will go dry.

One year ago to the day, Nebraska became the 36th state of the union to ratify the 18th Amendment—only 13 months after it was passed by Congress—which prohibits the "manufacture, sale, or transportation of intoxicating liquors."

Prohibition protesters

But not consumption.

So Americans will still be able to drink—but they now have to get their booze through illegal means. And they sure will.

At the National Cathedral in Washington, DC, a prayer service is being held, attended by those who fought for the last few years to have the amendment passed, led by inspirational speaker and three-time failed presidential candidate, William Jennings Bryan. 59.

In the bars and saloons, as midnight draws closer, bartenders are saying,

❝ Drink up."

Cheers.

✻ JANUARY 25, 1920 ✻
MANHATTAN, NEW YORK CITY, NEW YORK

Dorothy Parker, 26, is clearing out her desk on her last day as *Vanity Fair's* drama critic.

She'd loved this job. She'd spent the past four years with Conde Nast publishing, first at *Vogue*. She was thrilled when she was moved up to *Vanity Fair*.

Two weeks ago, the editor-in-chief, Frank Crowninshield, 47, had invited her for tea and scones at the Plaza Hotel. **Dottie** thought she was going to get that raise she had asked for. Ha.

Crownie apologetically explained that the regular drama critic she had replaced, P. G. Wodehouse, 38, was returning, so she'd have to go, of course. He also just mentioned that Conde Nast, 46, wasn't happy that so many Broadway producers complained about her negative reviews of their plays. Saying that Billie Burke, 35, the actress-wife of impresario Flo Ziegfeld, 52, had "thick ankles" was hardly theatrical criticism. Ziegfeld was threatening to pull his advertising.

Well, critics are supposed to give bad reviews too. That's why they are "critics," **Parker** thought. As she ordered the most expensive dessert.

Back at her apartment, her husband, Eddie, 26, still getting over the war, was no help. **Parker** had called her best friend, *Vanity Fair* managing editor **Robert Benchley**, 30, at his home in Scarsdale. He had come right down on the next train.

Adding her firing to that of their colleague, Robert Sherwood, 23, who was replaced by Nast's children's piano teacher, showed **Parker** and **Benchley** a pattern that they weren't happy about.

In the office the next morning, **Benchley** had written his resignation. He explained to Crownie—who hadn't expected to lose a good managing editor—that the job wasn't worth having without his two colleagues.

Parker was astounded. **Benchley** has a wife and two sons in the suburbs. Gertrude, 30, said she would support her husband's decision, but she sure wasn't happy about it.

Parker told him,

❝ It was the greatest act of friendship I'd known."

So now, on her last day, taking everything she could with her from the office, leaving nothing but the scent of her favorite perfume, Coty's Chypre, behind, she was conjuring up all the free-lance ways she could keep writing and earning. Crownie had suggested working from home. But she didn't even know how to change a typewriter ribbon.

Two of their New York newspaper friends, the *Times* drama critic **Alexander Woollcott**, just turned 33, and the city's most-read columnist, **FPA**, 38, at the *Tribune*, with whom they lunch almost every day at the nearby Algonquin Hotel, have promised to promote them in their papers. That would get those New York publisher tongues wagging.

Because of his contract, **Benchley** has to stay on until the end of the month—he plans to go out with a piece, "The Social Life of the Newt." He is being replaced by Princeton grad Edmund "Bunny" Wilson, 24. All **Parker** remembers about him is that he had hit on her during his job interview.

Robert Benchley

❦ JANUARY 30, 1920 ❧
MANHATTAN, NEW YORK CITY, NEW YORK

Irish poet **William Butler Yeats**, 54, and his wife Georgie, 27, are enjoying the first few weeks of his American lecture tour. They have left their 11-month old daughter, Annie, back in Dublin with his sisters, and are looking forward to the freedom of traipsing around the United States for the next four months.

It is just sinking in that Prohibition started a couple of weeks ago, and they can't get a drink in this town. Or any town.

Georgie has met her father-in-law, the painter John Butler Yeats, 80, for the first time, and finds him charming. He's quite enamored of his new daughter-in-law as well, writing to **Willie's** sister back in Ireland that Georgie has "no vast depths…[but] endless kindness and sympathy and I fancy a lot of practical talent."

Tonight the **Yeatses** are probably going to attend the Metropolitan Opera's *Oberon or The Elf King's Oath*, which their friend, Irish-American lawyer and art collector, John Quinn, 49, has recommended. They are excited about seeing the performance by the fantastic Rosa Ponselle, just turned 23, one of the Met's top young stars.

Rosa Ponselle

❧ FIRST WEEK OF FEBRUARY, ❧
1920
8 RUE DUPUYTREN, LEFT BANK, PARIS

After two and a half months of running her own bookshop, Shakespeare & Company, on the Left Bank of Paris, American Sylvia Beach, 32, daughter of a Princeton, New Jersey, Presbyterian minister, is having a ball.

She is writing to her sister Holly, 35, back in the States, about her new best friend forever, Adrienne Monnier, 27, owner of the bookstore, La Maison des Amis des Livres, a few blocks away. Adrienne and other Parisians were so helpful to Sylvia last fall in sorting out the details of starting a business in France. Adrienne and she had had "a sort of set-to or climax effect one day," she writes to Holly. Mostly about the design of the new bookshop. But now they have made up and

❝ become the best of friends…Adrienne is the best friend in the world and we get along puffickly [*sic*] now."

Beach loves the independence of having her own successful business—her lending library is up to 80 subscribers now—as well as getting to know the American and British ex-patriates who feel comfortable hanging out at her shop.

But the best part is being in the center of the creative life of the Left Bank. The two friends have been going to concerts and plays all over town. They've had fascinating lunch guests such as Parisian playwright Georges Duhamel, 35, and composer Erik Satie, 53. His compositions are so *funny*.

Satie mentioned that he is working on a project now with fellow French composer Darius Milhaud, 21, for a big performance being staged by poet Jean Cocteau, 30, later this month. But Satie is so secretive about all his work. Even when collaborating with Milhaud, he sent him a note saying,

❝ Don't give anything away. Not a word to ANYBODY, above all: Don't give anything away. SERIOUS."

Sylvia Beach

Sylvia, Adrienne, and some of their French friends—she is the only "foreigner" in the group—are planning to see Duhamel's hit play, *L'Oeuvre des athletes (The Action of Athletes)*, at the Theatre du Vieux-Colombier.

Beach suspects she is being included, not just because of her friendship with Monnier, but because the French like to ask her questions about one of her favorite American writers, the late Walt Whitman.

Sylvia writes to her sister,

❝ I am so lucky to be able to do something interesting [for] the rest of my life."

❧ FEBRUARY, 1920 ❧
MONTGOMERY, ALABAMA

Well. That was a scare. Zelda Sayre, 19, had been late.

Not late to the dance. Late.

Her current boyfriend, writer **F. Scott Fitzgerald**, 23, is back in New York City, finishing off his first novel to be published by Charles Scribner's Sons next month, and sending his short stories to magazines. **Scott** and Zelda were engaged. And then un-engaged.

He is still showering her with lots of presents.

When Zelda had written to tell him that she was late, **Scott** had sent her some pills to get rid of the unwanted baby.

Zelda Sayre

Zelda threw them away. Only prostitutes have abortions. Not socially prominent daughters of Southern judges.

She wrote back to **Scott**—or "Goofo" as she calls him—to say that "God—or something" would fix everything.

Must have been God.

She isn't late anymore.

❧ FEBRUARY, 1920 ❧
BLOOMSBURY, LONDON

Painter **Duncan Grant**, 35, is feeling pretty good about himself. His first solo show opened earlier this month at the Paterson-Carfax Gallery in Old Bond Street and sales are going well.

His Bloomsbury friends have been very supportive. Art critic **Roger Fry**, 53, organized the opening party. **Fry** picked **Duncan's** drawing *Reclining Nude* to give to their friend, novelist **Virginia Woolf**, 37, as a present, and **Duncan** gave her one of his watercolors. He's produced a lot of them this year.

Their other friend, another Bloomsbury resident, **Lytton Strachey**, 39, who just had a big hit with his untraditional biography, *Eminent Victorians*, bought **Grant's** painting *Juggler and Tightrope Walker* for £60.

Duncan Grant

Without revealing that he and **Duncan** are good friends, art critic **Clive Bell**, 38, **Virginia's** brother-in-law, had declared in the *Athenaeum*:

❝ **Duncan Grant** is, in my opinion, the best English painter alive."

Duncan has heard that the *Daily Telegraph's* critic is planning a less-than complementary review. But—at least his mom is happy. Ethel Grant, 57, wrote to him the day after the opening,

❝ I was a proud woman yesterday…Your show is going to be a big success I am convinced. You will know that five pictures were sold when we got there…I think the pictures are so well hung and when I went in the morning, with a bright sun and an empty room, the whole place seemed full of colour and joy. I felt exhilarated. Dear darling boy I am so pleased and hope you are going to make your mark at once."

Fingers crossed.

❧ FEBRUARY 16, 1920 ❧
PITTSBURGH, PENNSYLVANIA

One month after the Volstead Act took effect, prohibiting the sale and distribution of alcohol throughout the country, the wets' predictions of increased crime are coming true.

Pittsburgh is described in a government report, as

❝   wringing wet...Pennsylvania is very wet and only the price is needed by those who want whiskey and plenty of it."

Almost 300 doctors in the area have legal prescription pads to write their patients medicinal whiskey orders.

A popular mixture of creosote, denatured wood alcohol, and caramel coloring is known as "Pittsburgh Scotch."

The posh William Penn Hotel in downtown opens a speakeasy under the lobby with a secret escape route to Oliver Avenue in case of a raid, while the Dry Federation of Pennsylvania holds meetings upstairs. The nearby Nixon Theatre also has a speakeasy called "Flying Squadron," where jazz singer Helen Morgan, 20, performs on top of the piano.

The U. S. attorney John D. Meyer tells the Pittsburgh *Press*,

❝   If necessary, I will put a spy on every doorstep in Pittsburgh."

In the South Side flats section of the city, state representative Thomas J. Gallagher, 36, and his wife Flossie Cleis Gallagher, 35, welcome their seventh child, Virginia Mary Gallagher, my mother.

Pittsburgh in 1920

✣ FEBRUARY **21, 1920** ✣
5, HOLLAND PLACE CHAMBERS
KENSINGTON WEST, LONDON

American poet Ezra Pound, 35, is writing to his friend in New York City, Irish-American lawyer and supporter of art and artists, John Quinn, 49:

" Dear Quinn:

...Am writing this at [the home of illustrator Edmund Dulac] where I have brought my typewriter in hope of finishing an article before tomorrow a.m.,...Fool Dulac is playing the pianola upstairs in the inane belief that it can't be heard down here. As a matter of fact it wd. prevent me thinking out article if I weren't making more noise with Corona on unpadded dining table. ANYHOW combination of harmonies makes consecutive thought impossible...

If I get to Venice I shall, naturally, try to get up to Trieste to see [James] Joyce. Unless the serbo-slovocroats are firing broadsides...

I have arranged two amusing meetings in course of past week, one between [author Major Clifford Hughes] Douglas and [Wickham] Steed, edtr. of the Times (and intelligent), second between D[ouglas]. and **[John Maynard] Keynes**, who is an ass. Latter reason probably why his book is so much advertised, can't possibly do any damage to high finance. **Keynes'** style appalling, picture of Woodrow [Wilson] merely what I cd. have told him five or six yrs. ago...

John Maynard Keynes

Joyce has sent on another chapter ["Nausicaa" from *Ulysses*], excellent start but think he gets a bit too too too at the end of it. Have suggested slight alterations…Perhaps everything ought to be said ONCE in the English language. At least J[oyce]. seems bent on saying it…Who am I to tamper with a work of genius. For bigod genius it is in parts…

My regards to the **Yeats** family [touring America]. (Mrs. Y. approves of you, but of very little else save the architecture.)

yours ever

E. P."

❧ FEBRUARY **28, 1920** ❧
COMÉDIE DES CHAMPS-ÉLYSÉES
15 AVENUE MONTAIGNE, PARIS

Curtain going up—again! The *Premiere Spectacle-Concert* staged by poet Jean Cocteau, 30, is about to be presented for the fourth and probably last time. It's been more successful than the performers expected, when they premiered about a week ago in front of a carefully selected audience. A patron had bought up all the box seats: Cocteau didn't want the kind of nasty reaction that greeted the premier of *The Rite of Spring* by Igor Stravinsky, 37, at this theatre seven years ago.

Jean Cocteau

The *Premiere Spectacle-Concert* is a tribute to French culture, featuring the music of *Les Six,* particularly composer Erik Satie, 53. He has been working on his *Trois petites pièces montées (Three Little Stuffed Pieces)* for months now.

Some of the songs are set to some of Cocteau's own texts and two circus acrobats performing a fox trot. But the surprise hit has been the surrealist ballet by composer Darius Milhaud, 21. The dream sequence with the Fratellini clown family in slow motion contrasts with the outrageously fast music of this latest work, *Le Bœuf sur le toit, Op. 58 (The Ox on the Roof: The Nothing-Doing Bar).*

To hear Le Bœuf sur le toit, *see https://www.youtube.com/watch?v=BNkQXJwUOwQ. You'll recognize it.*

❧ MARCH 3, 1920 ❧
CASINO CLUB, CHICAGO, ILLINOIS

About six weeks in to his third American lecture tour, Irish poet **William Butler Yeats**, 54, is in Chicago, at a banquet given in his honor by *Poetry: A Magazine of Verse*, and its founder-editor, Harriet Monroe, 59.

Yesterday, the Chicago *Tribune* interviewed him over the phone when the reporter woke him in his hotel room after midnight. **Yeats** was quoted as saying,

"Musical Comedies? Never Saw One!"
Irish Poet and His Wife, Who Are Visiting Chicago on Lecture Tour of America.

MR. AND MRS. WILLIAM BUTLER YEATS.
(TRIBUNE Photo.)

The Yeatses in the Chicago Tribune

❝ I like Chicago, but Prohibition's hell, isn't it?"

Monroe had come right over to his room with

❝ a flagon of...surcease for your sorrow...I read in the *Tribune* this morning of your unpreparedness."

Yeats' talk at the banquet on "Poetic Drama" goes well. Arguing for smaller theatre companies and more intimate venues, he tells the crowd,

❝ I am trying to create a form of poetical drama played by one company, all of whom could ride in one taxicab and carry their stage properties on the roof."

Afterwards, back at the Auditorium Hotel, a group of reporters wake **Yeats** up and bring him down to their party in one of the private dining rooms. **Willie** perks up as soon as they offer him a glass of whiskey. And a second. And a third. His wife, Georgie, 27, soon shows up to drag him back to bed. On his way out, **Yeats** proclaims to the group,

❝ I will arise and go now, and go to Innisfree..."

❧ MARCH **10, 1920** ❧
BLOOMSBURY, LONDON

Painter **Vanessa Bell**, 40, is furious. And "amused." She has just received a letter from her friend, writer Madge Vaughan, 51, wife of her cousin, William, 55, the headmaster of quite posh Wellington College.

Vanessa and her sister, novelist **Virginia Woolf**, 38, have always been fond of Madge. But she definitely lives a much more traditional life than **Virginia** and **Vanessa** do.

Madge is interested in possibly renting out **Vanessa's** country home, Charleston in Sussex, for a family holiday, so she is staying there herself to try it out. Madge is well aware of **Vanessa's** bohemian living arrangements—with her husband, art critic **Clive Bell**, 38, her gay lover, painter **Duncan Grant**, 35, and their daughter, Angelica, 14 months old. But apparently actually being in the home with the well-blended **Bell** and **Grant** families makes Madge uncomfortable.

Vanessa Bell

In her letter to **Vanessa** she says,

    " I love you and I am *faithful* to old friends…I have set my back against slander and chatter and fought your battles always through the years. But I love, with increasing passion, *Goodness, purity and homeliness and the hearts of little children are the holiest things I know on earth.* And a question gnaws at my poor heart here in this house. It came stabbing my heart that day when I saw Angelica. I would like to meet you as a woman friend face to face at some quiet place and to talk it out. I don't feel I could come and live here with Will and the children unless I had done this."

Vanessa writes back,

❝   Why on earth should my moral character have anything to do with the question of your taking Charleston or not? I suppose you don't always enquire into your landlords' character. However, take it or not as you like...As for the gossip about me,...I cannot conceive why you think it any business of yours. I am absolutely indifferent to anything the world may say about me, my husband or my children... [Neither **Clive** nor I] think much of the world's will or opinion, or that a 'conventional home' is necessarily a happy or good one, that my married life has not been full of restraints but, on the contrary, full of ease, freedom and complete confidence..."

Thanks to Peter Monteith, Assistant Archivist at King's College, Cambridge, for help with dating these letters.

❧ MARCH 16, 1920 ❧
8 RUE DE DUPUYTREN, LEFT BANK, PARIS

Sylvia Beach, just turned 33, is curious about the couple she sees walking towards her bookshop, Shakespeare & Company, on the Left Bank.

On the left is a stout, tall woman, about 200 pounds, in rustic clothes, her head styled with a double bun that resembles a basket. Next to her is a smaller woman, dark-haired, thin, like a bird, with drooping eyes, a hooked nose, and the trace of a mustache, in gypsy-like clothes.

As they get closer, Sylvia recognizes them as American writer **Gertrude Stein**, 46, and her constant companion, **Alice B. Toklas**, 42.

Sylvia is familiar with **Stein's** works, *Tender Buttons* and *Three Lives*. And of course she has heard talk of the salons the two women have held at their home, 27 rue de Fleurus, on the other side of the Jardin du Luxembourg. Before the Great War, the local painters would come. Now, the Left Bank community is still reorganizing after the Armistice, and Sylvia has been so busy opening her shop, she hasn't yet sought out her fellow Americans.

So here comes **Stein** for her inaugural visit to Shakespeare & Company to sign up as a subscriber—not the first. The 91st.

During their chat, Beach mentions that she would welcome more

Gertrude Stein and Alice B. Toklas

American and British customers. **Stein** promises that she will help by sending out a flyer to all their friends.

A few days later, Sylvia sees the promotion which **Stein** has written which **Toklas** has typed up and mailed out:

> *Rich and Poor in English...*
> 66   The poor are remarkably represented...
> In dealing with money we can be funny..."

With the cost for book rentals listed on the back.

Beach feels that **Stein's** subscription is

> 66   merely a friendly gesture. She took little interest of course in any but her own books."

But, like many of Shakespeare & Company's visitors over this past year, **Gertrude** and **Alice** really like the atmosphere in the store.

❧ MARCH 22, 1920 ❧
FIRST CONGREGATIONAL CHURCH
TACOMA, WASHINGTON

Well in to his third American speaking tour, Irish poet **William Butler Yeats**, 54, is giving his second lecture in the state of Washington.

The Tacoma *Daily Ledger*, in addition to reporting the arrest of a top Seattle police officer for importing illegal booze from Canada, promotes **Yeats'** talk by indicating he will discuss his experiences hypnotizing dogs and cows.

Instead, **Willie** talks about his fellow founder of the Abbey Theatre, the late Irish playwright **John Millington Synge**, discusses the continuing achievements of the Abbey, and once again makes a plea for intimate theatre, "of the people, by the people, and for the people."

John Millington Synge

The 400 or so attendees are delighted by the poet's easy-going charm, particularly when **Yeats** follows his lecture by reading, as the paper reports the next day,

❝ three whimsical little poems that delighted…The poet's own personality was the dominant element in the lecture last night…He is an artist in feature, in dress and in gesture."

❧ BEFORE MARCH 26, 1920 ❧
153-157 FIFTH AVENUE
NEW YORK CITY, NEW YORK

The excitement is palpable. Employees at publishing house Charles Scribner's Sons are finally getting pumped up about the debut novel by **F. Scott Fitzgerald**, 23, the hot new discovery of Scribner's editor Maxwell Perkins, 35.

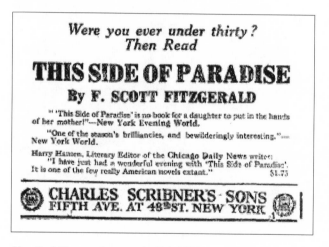

New York Times *ad, to run April 4, 1920*

Max's enthusiasm for *This Side of Paradise* had not initially been shared by his co-workers. After all, this **Fitzgerald** was the youngest novelist Scribner's had ever published.

When one of the men in the sales department had any doubts about a new book, he would take it home for his well-educated sister to read. She had proved to be a good predictor of success. So his fellow employees were all eager to know what she had thought of *Paradise*. He reported,

> ❝ She picked it up with tongs because she wouldn't touch it with her hands after reading it, and put it into the fire."

Perkins was so worried about negative reactions within the house, that he tried to keep the manuscript mostly in his own hands. As a former

Scribner's advertising director, he had approved the upcoming ad to run in the New York *Times*.

Perkins didn't even want the staff proofreaders to have a crack at the novel. As a result, he knows that the printed version will be riddled with typos. Even more embarrassing to Perkins is that **Fitzgerald**—a terrible speller himself—is pointing out mistakes to him.

As publication day approaches, Perkins wonders if he has done the right thing by fighting to have tradition-encrusted Scribner's take on this new writing.

✤ MARCH 27 AND 28, 1920 ✤
NEW YORK CITY, NEW YORK;
HOLLYWOOD, CALIFORNIA;
AND MONTGOMERY, ALABAMA

Jane Grant and Harold Ross

Harold Ross, 27, who has made a name for himself around the publishing world by being the successful editor of the U. S. Army's newspaper, *The Stars & Stripes*, in Paris during the Great War, is doing quite well now that he is state-side. **Ross** has just signed a contract to become editor of the *American Legion Weekly*, the house organ for veterans adjusting to their new lives back in the States.

The contract is his wedding present to Jane Grant, also 27, who he is secretly eloping with later today.

Ross and Grant met in Paris during the war, when she was there with the American Red Cross, entertaining soldiers.

They had discussed marriage a few times, and this week she said to him,

❝ How about Saturday?"

So he agreed.

They plan to live on Grant's salary as the first full-time female reporter for the New York *Times*, and save **Ross'** earnings to start the magazine about New York that they are planning.

✂✁✂

The next day, the rest of the country is thrilled with a different wedding. "America's Sweetheart," Mary Pickford, 27, is marrying her co-star, "Everybody's Hero," Douglas Fairbanks, 36. The worst kept secret in the movie business is that their affair began while they were each married to others. But America is willing to forgive their beloved "Hollywood Royalty." The Fairbanks are off to Europe for their honeymoon.

✂✁✂

Down south in Montgomery, Alabama, Zelda Sayre, 19, is planning for her wedding. The handsome young soldier she met during the war when he was stationed nearby at Camp Sheridan, **F. Scott Fitzgerald**, 23, now living in New York City, has been wooing her with love letters and presents: An ostrich fan. His mother's ring. A diamond and platinum watch. They were nice. But what really did the trick is when he signed a contract with Charles Scribner's Sons to publish his first novel, *This Side of Paradise*. And Metro Studios bought the film rights to one of his short stories for $2,500.

That's when Zelda said yes.

The novel was published this week and she's getting ready for the wedding in early April.

❧ EARLY APRIL, 1920 ❧
ALGONQUIN HOTEL, 59 WEST 44TH STREET
NEW YORK CITY, NEW YORK

Well, this should be interesting, thinks free-lance writer **Dorothy Parker**, 26.

Her friend and former co-worker at *Vanity Fair*, Robert Sherwood, just turned 24, now managing editor at *Life* magazine, has invited her and one of her many escorts, Edmund "Bunny" Wilson, also 24, for a special lunch at the Algonquin Hotel. He wants them all to meet first-time novelist **F. Scott Fitzgerald**, 23, and his new wife Zelda, 19.

Dorothy Parker

Instead of the Rose Room, where **Parker** and Sherwood regularly lunch with their fellow New York writers these days, today they are in the smaller Oak Room, just off the lobby, to avoid the crowds. All five are squeezed into a banquette, lined up against the wall. The food is identical to that in the main dining room: $1.65 for the Blue Plate Special—broiled chicken, cauliflower with hollandaise, beets with butter, fried potatoes, and the same free popovers.

They have all run into each other a few times before. But this is the first chance **Parker** has to size up Zelda, this Southern belle **Scott** has been talking about endlessly. Except when he's talking about the fabulous sales of his first novel, *This Side of Paradise*.

Apparently, he hasn't yet read the latest review by one of **Parker's** other writer-friends, **Heywood Broun**, 31, in the New York *Tribune*, which called **Fitzgerald's** writing "complacent...pretentious...self-conscious...[and the main characters] male flappers." Their other lunch-buddy, **FPA**, 38, has made a game in his *Tribune* column of spotting typos throughout the novel.

Dottie tunes out **Scott's** youthful enthusiasm to focus on his new bride. Not quite as frivolous as **Parker** expected. Zelda sports the latest, fashionable bobbed hair, chews gum, and speaks in a predictable southern drawl. **Parker** has seen that Kewpie-doll face many times before.

And Zelda is sizing up **Mrs. Parker**, professional writer. Long hair. Big hat. Condescending. Boring, Zelda decides.

❧ APRIL **10, 1920** ❧
MONK'S HOUSE, RODMELL, EAST SUSSEX, ENGLAND

Novelist **Virginia Woolf**, 38, and her husband, **Leonard**, 39, are getting accustomed to life in their new country home, the 18th century cottage they bought at auction just last year.

Today she confides to her diary,

> ❝ We only slept by snatches last night, and at 4 am turned a mouse out of **Leonard's** bed. Mice crept and rattled all night through. Then the wind got up. Hasp of the window broke. Poor **Leonard** out of bed for the fifth time to wedge it with a toothbrush. So I say nothing about our projects at Monks, though the view across the meadows to Caburn is before me now; and the hyacinths blooming, and the orchard walk. Then being alone there—breakfast in the sun—posts—no servants—how nice it all is!"

Virginia is working on her third novel and is thinking that she and **Leonard** could publish this one themselves through their own five-year-old Hogarth Press. That would be better than having to submit her work again to Gerald Duckworth & Co., owned by her half-brother.

Monk's House

❧ APRIL **15, 1920** ☙
BRAINTREE, MASSACHUSETTS

At the Slater & Morrill Shoe Co. on Pearl Street, the company paymaster and a security guard are walking with the payroll to the main building.

Two armed men grab the metal boxes holding more than $15,000, shoot the guard four times as he reaches for his gun, and shoot the other, unarmed, man in the back as he tries to run away.

Three other men pull up in a dark blue Buick. The robbers jump in and keep shooting out the window as the car speeds them away.

Slater & Morrill Shoe Co., Braintree, Massachusetts

❧ APRIL **19, 1920** ❧
LEFT BANK, PARIS

Eleanor Beach, 56, is on her annual visit to see her daughters—she calls them her "chicks"—who live in Europe.

The youngest, Sylvia, 33, owns an English-language bookshop and lending library in Paris on the rue Dupuytren, Shakespeare & Company, which seems to be going well. It hasn't even been open a year and she already has 103 subscribers to the lending library, most of whom are pretty active borrowers.

But Mom wants to help out. So she and her daughter go on a shopping spree and come back with some decent clothes, a kitchen table, and some more books for the shop.

Sylvia writes to her sister, Holly, 35, in Florence, Italy,

❝ PLM [Poor Little Mother] is flourishing."

Sylvia's good friend, Adrienne Monnier, 27, who owns a French-language bookshop a few blocks away, La Maison des Amis des Livres, has been a big help in Sylvia's first year in business.

Adrienne Monnier and Sylvia Beach

Shakespeare & Company recently had good write-ups in the respected trade journal *Publisher's Weekly* and other English-language publications distributed in France. As a result, Sylvia is having a hard time responding to all the letters she is receiving. Many American students write asking for jobs. Sylvia is feeling more like a secretary, rather than an entrepreneur.

❧ BEFORE APRIL 24, 1920 ❧
EAST LONDON

Jamaican Claude McKay, 30, probably the only working Black journalist in Britain, is looking forward to seeing his letter to the editor in one of the newspapers he writes for, the *Workers' Dreadnought*, founded and edited by noted activist Sylvia Pankhurst, 37, daughter of Suffragette Emmaline, 61.

He knows that "A Black Man Replies" will be the headline. The inflammatory piece is the strongest shot in a battle between the Communist Party's *Dreadnought* and the Labour Party's *Daily Herald*, edited by George Lansbury, 61, a former Labour Member of Parliament.

April 24, 1920.

A BLACK MAN REPLIES.

Dear Editor: The following letter, replying to E. D. Morel's article on the black troops in Germany, was sent to the *Daily Herald* on April 11th, but apparently the *Herald* refuses a hearing to the other side, which is quite inarticulate :—
The Editor of the *Daily Herald*.
    Sir: The odiousness of your article headlined "Black Scourge in Europe; Sexual Horror let loose" is not mitigated by your explanatory editorial and note stating that you are not encouraging race prejudice and that you champion native rights in Africa.

Claude McKay's article in the Workers' Dreadnought

Earlier in the month, the *Herald* had run an article by E. D. Morel, 46, "Black Scourge in Europe: Sexual Horror Let Loose by France on the Rhine," about French troops from northern Africa based in Germany after the Great War.

McKay had sent his reply to the *Herald* the very next day. But Lansbury had ignored it. Pankhurst, however, is proud to publish it—even though Lansbury has often helped out her enterprise by supplying money to buy newsprint when she needed it. But she's criticized him publicly before.

McKay writes,

❝   Why this obscene maniacal outburst about the sex vitality of Black men in a proletarian paper? Rape is rape; the colour of the skin doesn't make it different...I do not protest because I happen to be a Negro...I write because I feel that the ultimate result of your propaganda will be further strife and blood-spilling between whites and the many members of my race."

McKay is outraged. This over-sexualizing of Black men is what he would have expected from some publication of the Ku Klux Klan in America. His years living there had opened his eyes to racism. How could an important national left-wing newspaper like the *Herald* publish hateful, racist articles like Morel's?

Sylvia is proud of her adopted East London neighbourhood, brimming with immigrants and sailors off the ships which dock here. McKay writes that he has been told by white men in the neighbourhood, "who ought to know, that this summer will see a recrudescence of the outbreaks that occurred last year."

In other words, more attacks on people of color.

❧ 150 YEARS AGO ❧
APRIL 24, 1870
TIFFIN, OHIO

Happy birthday, John Quinn! We interrupt our documenting of events that happened 100 years ago with a momentous event of 150 years ago.

You may have seen John Quinn's name in these pages and wondered who he is. Hosting Irish poet **William Butler Yeats** and his wife in New York. Writing and receiving letters to and from American ex-patriate poet Ezra Pound. Buying up manuscripts of works by writers like **Yeats**, Joseph Conrad and James Joyce.

John Quinn

This is a posting I wrote in 2003 about Quinn in my weekly blog, *Every Wednesday: The Journal of a Teacher in Search of a Classroom*, chronicling my year of unemployment in south Florida. [Available on Lulu.com.]

Every Wednesday: I Want to Tell You About an Amazing Man

When I was doing my research for my dissertation on early 20th century writers' salons there was this character who kept popping up. Like Woody Allen's Zelig he appeared in biographies, memoirs and letters of the time, as well as in group photos of people like **Yeats**, Picasso, Matisse, Ezra Pound, James Joyce. Who was this guy? He certainly had "such friends."

When I first came across Quinn, I checked the bibliographies and saw that there was one biography about him, B. L. Reid's *The Man from New York: John Quinn and His Friends* (New York: Oxford University Press, 1968). Earlier this year I began doing some research on the 1913 New York Armory Show to include in my work-in-progress about the writers' salons. There was John Quinn again, buying art in Paris, organizing the first exhibition of international modern art in the United States, corresponding with Conrad and other struggling writers of the time.

Jealous that someone else had written the definitive history of this intriguing person, I broke down and took the biography out of the library. I discovered that it's not great—good research but not well-presented, hard to read. And, worst of all, the author makes this fascinating man's life seem boring.

So here is the John Quinn I discovered. I'm still working on some of the details.

He was born in Tiffin, Ohio, on this date in 1870 of Irish immigrant parents; his father was a baker. He grew up in middle-class Fostoria, Ohio, and attended the University of Michigan. A family friend who became Secretary of the Treasury under President Benjamin Harrison offered him a job in Washington, DC. While working full-time in the federal government, he went to Georgetown University law school at night. After receiving his law degree, he earned an advanced degree in international relations from Harvard University. Not bad for the son of a shanty-Irish baker.

Quinn then moved to New York City, which was to be his home for the rest of his life. He predictably got a job with a major New York law firm and worked on a lot of high profile corporate cases. During a two-year period there were a lot of deaths in his family—parents, sisters, etc.—and he began to explore his Irish roots.

Right after the turn of the century he went to Ireland and, while attending a Gaelic language festival in the west, near Galway, met **Lady Augusta Gregory** and other friends of **Yeats** involved in the Irish Literary Renaissance. While helping them found the Abbey Theatre, he started his own law firm in 1906. As you do.

❧ SPRING, 1920 ❧
OFFICES OF *LIFE* MAGAZINE
NEW YORK CITY, NEW YORK

Robert Sherwood

New drama critic **Robert Benchley**, 30, is rested from his recent family vacation and ready to start his latest job.

For the past year or so, **Benchley** was managing editor of *Vanity Fair* magazine. But when his two friends and critics, **Dorothy Parker**, 26, and Robert Sherwood, just turned 24, were let go earlier this year, he decided that job wasn't worth having. **Benchley** was replaced by nervous Edmund "Bunny" Wilson, 24, whom he considered to be a scab. But he agreed to train him anyway.

Parker and **Benchley** had jumped right into free-lancing, and even rented a tiny office together for $30 a month, above the Metropolitan Opera House at Broadway and 39th Street.

As **Parker** described it,

❝ One cubic foot less of space and it would have constituted adultery."

The free-lance offers have come pouring in, for both of them. **Benchley** is still doing his "Books and Other Things" column three times a week for the New York *World*, for the same money as his full-time *Vanity Fair* job paid.

But **Benchley** has a wife and two sons—aged 5 and 1—up in Scarsdale. So when Sherwood recently became associate editor of humor magazine *Life*, circulation 250,000, and offered **Benchley** a full-time drama critic position, he jumped at it. $100 a week—great!

And his wife understands that he will have to stay in town with **Parker** and Sherwood most nights to see plays. He is keeping his formal clothes in the office.

Back in their old office, **Dottie** has put a sign on the door that says "MEN."

❧ MAY 5, 1920 ❧
BROCKTON, MASSACHUSETTS

Brockton trolley

The police have been waiting for weeks. The getaway car, used last month in the brutal burglary and double murder at a shoe factory in nearby Braintree, had shown up at a garage here. They know that eventually someone will have to come by to pick it up, and the garage owner has agreed to alert the cops.

Today, four men come to get the dark blue Buick. When the garage keeper tries to delay them, two drive off on their motorcycles and the other two jump on to a streetcar headed for Brockton.

As soon as the cops stop the trolley, they know they have their men. Two Italian immigrants, Nicola Sacco, 29, and Bartolomeo Vanzetti, 31. They match the descriptions given by witnesses, they're carrying pistols, they have no good alibis for the day of the murders. And they deny being anarchists— just before the cops find a flyer in Sacco's pocket announcing an anarchist lecture by Vanzetti.

Guilty!

❧ MAY, 1920 ❧
244 COMPO ROAD SOUTH
WESTPORT, CONNECTICUT

Newlywed Zelda Sayre Fitzgerald, 19, is bored. She is sitting on the beach not far from their rented, colonial-style 150-plus-year old house, where her new husband, hit novelist **F. Scott Fitzgerald**, 24, is upstairs writing short stories. Always writing.

Of course, he gets about $900 for each one, like "Bernice Bobs Her Hair" in this month's *Saturday Evening Post*, so at least that will pay some bills.

Zelda Fitzgerald at Compo Beach, Connecticut

Their local bootlegger, Baldy Jack Rose, 43, keeps them in cheap whiskey. And their mysterious next store neighbour, Frederick Lewis, is a thirty-ish multimillionaire who pretty much keeps to himself. He doesn't mind if Zelda shortcuts across his property to get to the beach, which makes the 20-minute walk a bit more interesting. And he gives great parties.

But Zelda is still bored. When **Scott's** not working they drive their sports car around the countryside, or back into the city. Although, since she ran over a fire hydrant, **Scott** won't let her behind the wheel anymore.

They finally had to hire a Japanese house boy for the cleaning and cooking because Zelda sure as heck couldn't do any of *that*.

She thought that finally getting out of Montgomery, Alabama, away from her family, moving up north, getting married—she thought it would all be more exciting than this.

Now she spends most days hungover, sipping lemonade, sitting in a beach chair. Looking across the Sound to Long Island.

Thanks to Richard Webb at Gatsby in Connecticut *[https://gatsbyinct.com/] for help in authenticating details of this post.*

❧ MAY, 1920 ❧
ALGONQUIN HOTEL, 59 WEST 44TH STREET
NEW YORK CITY, NEW YORK

Eamon de Valera

Poet **William Butler Yeats**, 54, and his wife Georgie, 28, are settling into New York City. They have spent this whole year so far on **Willie's** third American lecture tour. It's been a big success, but they're exhausted.

Their dear friend, Irish-American lawyer and supporter of the arts, John Quinn, just turned 50, really wants them to stay with him in his spacious Central Park West apartment. They will—but they decided that a few days at the Algonquin Hotel first will be more restful.

They are only planning to be in New York for a couple of weeks before they head for Montreal to board the *Megantic* back to England. Quinn has arranged all their tickets and transportation.

Someone has offered to record **Yeats** for "a new kind of moving picture—a picture that talks as well as moves," as he describes it.

Quinn says they might have the opportunity to meet an Irish politician also touring America. Eamon de Valera, 37, self-proclaimed President of Dáil

Éireann, the Parliament of the new Irish Republic, has asked to meet his country's most famous poet. And **Yeats** is curious—is this former Irish rebel just all propaganda? Or is there a real human in there?

Mostly, they plan to spend more time with **Willie's** father, painter John Butler Yeats, 81, whom Quinn has been keeping an eye on ever since he moved from Dublin to Manhattan 13 years ago. He was supposed to stay just a few weeks!

The Yeats family had implored their father to come home to Ireland. But J. B. had written to **Yeats** that, as an American had pointed out,

❝   In Dublin it is hopeless insolvency. Here it is hopeful insolvency."

And so he stayed.

❧ MAY 14, 1920 ❧
HOME MARKET CLUB, BOSTON, MASSACHUSETTS

Candidate for the Republican presidential nomination Ohio Senator Warren G. Harding, 54, has just finished his speech before the Home Market Club, publisher of *The Protectionist* magazine.

His campaign manager, Harry Daugherty, 60, had urged him to go ahead with this speech. They were both very disappointed by the results of last month's Ohio primary. He won his own state by only 15,000 votes, gaining only 39 out of the 48 delegates. And then he came in fourth in Indiana with no delegates at all.

A fortune teller had told his wife Florence, 59, that Warren would become president and then die in office, but both Florence and Harry had convinced him to stay in the race anyway.

In his speech, Harding told the conservative crowd,

❝ My countrymen, there isn't anything the matter with world civilization, except that humanity is viewing it through a vision impaired in a cataclysmal war. Poise has been disturbed, and nerves have been racked, and fever has rendered men irrational…America's present need is not heroics, but healing; not nostrums, but normalcy… If we can prove [to be] a representative popular government under which a citizenship seeks what it may do for the government and country rather than what the country may do for individuals, we shall do more to make democracy safe for the world than all armed conflict ever recorded…My best judgment of America's need is to steady down, to get squarely on our feet…Let's get out of the fevered delirium of war…"

Harding will record this and all his speeches for sale as phonographic discs.

To listen to Harding's full "Return to Normalcy" speech—only five minutes long—on the Library of Congress site, see https://www.loc.gov/item/2016655168/

❧ MAY 29, 1920 ❧
ATLANTA FEDERAL PENITENTIARY
ATLANTA, GEORGIA

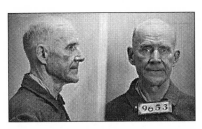

Eugene V. Debs mug shot

One year in to his 10-year sentence for sedition, Eugene V. Debs, 64, pulls off a coup. He accepts the nomination of the Socialist Party for president of the United States. For the fifth time.

When Debs ran eight years ago, he got 6% of the vote, the most for any Socialist Party candidate ever. In Florida, he even came in ahead of the incumbent Republican president.

This November will be the first time when women are able to vote in federal elections—assuming the 19th Amendment is finally ratified by the last few states, as expected. There will be more voters than ever.

Debs had been imprisoned last year after being found guilty of making a speech urging men to resist the draft during the Great War.

He proudly wears his prison uniform when formally accepting the nomination. Knowing he will not be able to make any campaign addresses or even statements. And that his full sentence will not be over until after the next two presidential administrations.

But part of his platform is that, if elected, he will pardon himself.

❧ JUNE 1, 1920 ❧
SIRMIONE, LAGO DI GARDA, NORTHERN ITALY

American poet Ezra Pound, 34, looking out on a lake in northern Italy, is writing to his benefactor, American lawyer and art collector, John Quinn, 50, in New York City.

He thanks Quinn for having negotiated a deal for Pound to serve as foreign editor for the American literary magazine, *The Dial*. He mentions that the magazine had already sent him a check for 2,050 lire, about $100, drawn on a Genoa bank. But no one in this part of the country wants to cash it.

Then he writes about their mutual friend, Irish poet **William Butler Yeats**, 54, recently returned from his third American lecture tour, which had problems with the tour promotion agency:

Yeats' tower in the west of Ireland, Thoor Ballylee, flooded

❝ —Poor **W. B. Y.** perhaps he'll now settle down & lead an honest life—Am sorry for his ill fortune but can't feel he's wholly spotless, he that went forth to gall the ignorant... Besides he'll have made enough to buy a few shingles for his phallic symbol on the Bogs. Bally phallus or whatever he calls it with the river on the first floor."

❧ SUMMER, 1920 ❧
LONDON, BISHOPSBOURNE,
AND EAST SUSSEX, ENGLAND

At 74 Gloucester Place in Marylebone, London, publisher and editor Harriet Shaw Weaver, 43, is thrilled to have received a letter from the American owner of the Paris bookshop, Shakespeare & Company, Sylvia Beach, 33.

Beach wants to buy as many books by Irish writer James Joyce, 38, as she can from Weaver's Egoist Press, which supports Joyce. Weaver is writing back to offer Shakespeare & Company a 33% discount and free shipping. She knows this is going to be a good deal.

Later in the summer, Weaver uses an inheritance from her aunt to set up a trust to fund Joyce. She had submitted his latest work in progress, *Ulysses*, to many publishers, including London's Hogarth Press, run by **Virginia Woolf**, 38, and her husband **Leonard**, 39, but no one wants to touch it.

Roger Fry

A few stops east on the Metropolitan Railway, and a short walk from Euston Station, a luncheon is being held at 46 Gordon Square in Bloomsbury to honor art critic and painter **Roger Fry**, 53, on the occasion of his private showing of 81 paintings at London's Independent Gallery. His Bloomsbury friend, fellow painter **Duncan Grant**, 35, has returned from his two-month trip to France and Italy with two cases of paintings that **Fry** had done while he was there.

Fry appreciates his friends' attempt to cheer him up because, despite fairly low prices for all his works, neither the reviews nor the sales are going well. Earlier in the summer he had written to a friend,

❝ It's almost impossible for an artist to live in England: I feel so isolated."

After an easy Underground ride from nearby Russell Square station, south on the Piccadilly Line to Leicester Square station, it's a short walk to the New Theater. The first play by actor Noel Coward, 20, *I'll Leave It to You*, is getting very good reviews. Coward stars in his own play, which has just transferred to the West End from a successful run up north in Manchester.

The London *Times* is excited:

❝ It is a remarkable piece of work from so young a head—spontaneous, light, and always 'brainy.'"

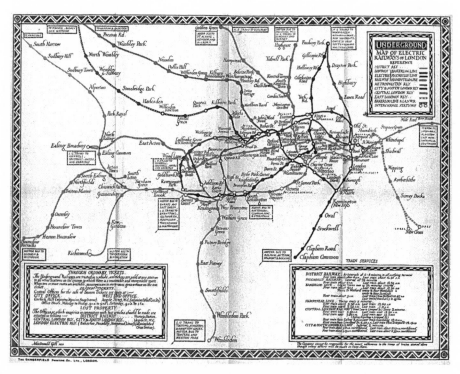

London Underground map

And the *Observer* predicts:

❝ Mr Coward...has a sense of comedy, and if he can overcome a tendency to smartness, he will probably produce a good play one of these days." But this one closes after only 37 performances.

From Leicester Square station, heading south down the Hampstead Line, changing to go east on the District Line, the Cannon Street station is in the heart of the City, the financial capital of the country. At the Cannon Street Hotel, a group of radical socialists have gathered for the first Congress of their newly formed Communist Party of Great Britain.

The publisher and editor of the socialist *Workers' Dreadnought* newspaper, Sylvia Pankhurst, 38, and one of her reporters, Jamaican Claude McKay, 30, both attend. But Sylvia decides the Communists are way too right wing for her taste, and votes against affiliating with the Labour Party.

Farther south down the District Line, near the West Kensington station, poet Ezra Pound, 34, is back in London after spending time in Europe specifically to introduce his new find, James Joyce, to the literary society of Paris. Pound gives a brown paper package with old clothing and shoes to his friends, poet T. S. Eliot, 31, and painter and writer Wyndham Lewis, 37, to pass on to Joyce on their upcoming trip to Paris.

Farther south, the District line terminates in Richmond. A few blocks from the station in Hogarth House on Paradise Road, the **Woolfs** are feeling overwhelmed by the success of their Hogarth Press.

The sales flooding in up until now have been primarily the result of word of mouth among their Bloomsbury friends. Who also send along their manuscripts for the **Woolfs** to publish.

They've recently taken their first ads in national papers such as the *Times* and the Manchester *Guardian* and magazines such as the *Nation* and the *New Statesman*. **Leonard** is closing out the account for Eliot's *Poems*, and finds they have made a small profit of £9.

This summer they are planning to bring out *Reminiscences of Count Leo Tolstoi*, by Maxim Gorky, 52, translated by their friend S.S. Koteliansky, 40.

This is quite a landmark for the **Woolfs** and their five-year-old company. Not only is it the first Russian translation they have published, with an initial run of 1,250, it is also the first time they have used an outside commercial printer from beginning to end. Up until now they have been setting type, printing and binding, all on their own in their home. Now they have become a true publishing house, not just a small press.

Virginia writes to a friend,

❝ The Hogarth Press is growing like a beanstalk and [**Leonard** and I] think we must set up a shop and keep a clerk."

Later in the summer she confides to her diary that **Leonard** is

❝ on the verge of destruction. As a hobby, the Hogarth Press is clearly too lively & lusty to be carried on in this private way any longer. Moreover, the business part of it can't be shared, owing to my incompetence. The future, therefore, needs consideration."

About a two-hour drive southeast of Richmond is Bishopsbourne, Kent. At his house, Oswalds, Polish-born novelist Joseph Conrad, 62, is writing to his American benefactor, Irish-American lawyer, John Quinn, 50, in New York.

Oswalds, Bishopsbourne, Kent

Quinn was not happy that Conrad went back on his promise to sell the manuscript of his latest novel to Quinn. But Conrad explained that he had hurriedly sold it to another collector to get cash quickly, and Quinn was understanding. Conrad writes,

❝ I am glad you take my arrangement as to the MSS. so well…I had many claims on me, and I have some still…—not to speak of my wife's prolonged disablement."

Conrad is comforted by the fact that after his death his copyrights will help support his wife Jessie, 46, and their two sons. One of whom is named for Quinn.

Quinn writes back to re-assure him,

❝ You are far from the end of your time…You are one of the leading writers living in the world today and still producing work that is worthy of your best…There is no falling off there [in Conrad's latest novel *The Rescue*]! It is a fine thing, one of your best things."

⁂

Seventy miles farther south, in Rodmell, East Sussex, the **Woolfs** are spending the last half of the summer at their country home, Monk's House, still worried about overworking at Hogarth.

Their young friends, painter Dora Carrington, 27, and her lover Ralph Partridge, 26, have come to stay for a weekend, and the **Woolfs** talk to Partridge about working for them. **Virginia** writes to **Fry**, back in Bloomsbury, that she and **Leonard** "now think of setting up a proper printing plant and doing all production ourselves—that is with a manager…[Or else close it] as we can't go on with it as we've been doing.'"

By the end of August the Hogarth Press has hired Partridge as a part-time assistant for £100 per year and 50% of their net profit.

A 20-minute drive away, at Charleston Farmhouse, **Virginia's** sister, painter **Vanessa Bell**, is hosting the usual summer assemblage of Bloomsbury creatives.

Julian, 12, her son with her estranged husband, art critic **Clive Bell**, 38, has set off his airgun by mistake and a bullet has gotten stuck in a chair.

According to one of their friends, **Clive** is "pretending to read Stendhal" up in his room.

Down the hall, economist **John Maynard Keynes**, just turned 37, is working on his latest book, *A Treatise on Probability*, while continuing to edit the *Economic Journal*.

Charleston Farmhouse, Firle, East Sussex

Vanessa and her partner, **Duncan Grant**, are working on a huge project. **Keynes** has commissioned them to create new murals for his rooms at King's College, Cambridge. They have decided to produce eight allegorical figures, alternating male and female, to fill almost a whole wall, representing Science, Political Economics, Music, Classics, Law, Mathematics, Philosophy and History. They are advising **Maynard** on every detail of the interior decoration of the sitting room, right down to the color of the curtains.

Duncan has just returned from a visit to his aging parents up in Kent, and is a bit concerned about his father's welfare. He tells **Vanessa** that in the nursing home the Major, 63, is "spending most of his time alone and hardly ever speaking at meals." **Duncan** hopes **Virginia** and **Leonard** could make use of his father on some Hogarth Press project.

Overall, **Duncan** writes to a friend back in Bloomsbury,

" Life here is very quiet."

✣ JUNE, 1920 ✣

ON A TRAIN BETWEEN MISSOURI AND TEXAS

Langston Hughes, 19, freshly graduated from Central High School in Cleveland, Ohio, has finished his dinner and is back in the Pullman car, looking out the window at the sunset over the mighty Mississippi.

On his way to visit his father in Toluca, Mexico—again—he is trying to figure out how to convince his dad to send him to Columbia University. Dad is willing to fund college if Langston goes abroad and studies engineering.

But mathematics is not Langston's strong suit. He's a writer. In high school he wrote for the newspaper and edited the yearbook. His favorite teacher, Miss Helen Maria Chestnutt, 40, encouraged him to write poetry, plays, short stories—anything.

One of Langston's first poems was written to a girl he met at a dance:

❝   …And the beauty of Susanna Jones in red
Burns in my heart a love-fire sharp like pain.
Sweet silver trumpets,
Jesus!"

Now he is mesmerized by the river, thinking of how his ancestors have been influenced by rivers throughout history. He thinks,

❝   I've known rivers."

Langston writes that sentence on the back of an envelope.

To hear Langston Hughes talk about and read his first famous poem, "The Negro Speaks of Rivers" [it's short], see https://www.youtube.com/watch?v=8cKDOGhghMU

❧ JUNE 12, 1920 ❧
THE COLISEUM, CHICAGO, ILLINOIS

The 940 delegates at the Republican National Convention have been through four long days and 10 long ballots. They finally have a compromise candidate, Ohio Senator Warren G. Harding, 54, the result of negotiations in what his supporters refer to as a "smoke filled room."

His plea for a "return to normalcy" in a recent speech had made him palatable to both the conservative and progressive wings of the party. Although he has been called "the best of the second-raters."

Baltimore *Sun* reporter H. L. Mencken, 39, has said that the smell in the overheated Coliseum is like that of a "third rate circus."

Sitting with the other reporters, Edna Ferber, 34 [but she only admits to 31], novelist, playwright and former full-time journalist, now

Edna Ferber

here on special assignment for the United Press, is melting in the heat. In one of her reports she has described how all the bald, sweating delegates had

❝ shed collars, ties, even shoes in some cases…It was the American male politician reduced to the most common denominator."

Ferber has been watching the spectacle and listening to the endless speakers. In his acceptance speech today, Harding says,

❝ We mean to be American first, to all the world…We must stabilize and strive for normalcy."

The country is just months away from having the 19th Amendment ratified by the last few states, and, for the first time, women will be able to vote in a presidential election. So, probably after the persuasion of his wife, Harding throws a bone to the suffragettes:

❝   By party edict, by my recorded vote, by personal conviction, I am committed to this measure of justice."

After suffering through Harding's speech, Ferber describes him thus:

❝   Here is a living cartoon of the American Fourth of July stuffed shirt order."

❧ JUNE 19, 1920 ❧
HOTEL ELYSEE, 3 RUE DE BEAUNE, PARIS

About ten days ago, when American poet Ezra Pound, 34, was still in Italy, he had met for the first time the Irish writer whom he had been corresponding with and encouraging for seven years, James Joyce, 38.

He had convinced Joyce to move the entire Joyce family to Paris in the next few months. Pound promised he will pave the way with the proper introductions.

James Joyce

Today he is writing to the American patron of the arts and artists, lawyer John Quinn, 50, back in New York, describing his first impressions of Joyce:

> ❝ Dear John Quinn:
>
> I came out of Italy on a tram-car [because of a rail strike] & reckon the next man will come out in a cab.
>
> Joyce finally got to Sirmione [Italy]; dont [*sic*] know yet whether he has got back to Trieste…

Joyce pleasing; after the first shell of cantankerous Irishman…

A concentration & absorption passing [that of **W. B. Yeats**, 55, who] has never taken on anything requiring the condensation of *Ulysses*.

—Also gt. exhaustion, but more constitution than I had expected, & apparently good recovery from eye operation.

He is coming up here later; long reasons but justified in taking a rest from Trieste.

He is of course as stubborn as a mule or an Irishman, but I failed to find him at all *unreasonable*: Thank god he has been stubborn enough to know his job & stick to it…

He is also dead right in refusing to interrupt his stuff by writing stray articles for cash. Better in the end, even from practical point of view…

In the stories of his early eccentricities in Dublin I have always thought people neglected the poignant feature: i.e. that his "outrageous" remarks were usually *so*.

His next work will go to the *Dial* [magazine]—but he shd. rest after *Ulysses*…

yours ever

E. P."

❧ JUNE, 1920 ❧
MANCHESTER *GUARDIAN*, ENGLAND

E ven though the influenza epidemic is ending, Pinkobolic soap still touts its properties as an efficient disinfectant which purifies.

❧ AFTER JUNE 20, 1920 ❧
MARION, OHIO

A strange presidential campaign. No rallies. No crowds. No door knocking. No hand shaking. No baby-kissing.

Warren Harding greeting crowds from his front porch

The candidate is staying at home, although making good use of new technology to communicate to voters.

Ohio Senator and recently nominated Republican presidential candidate Warren G. Harding, 54, has decided to run a "front porch campaign" like some of his predecessors in the late 19th century.

Marion, Ohio, has become a mecca for business leaders, politicians, supporters, protesters—and celebrities! Newlywed movie stars Mary Pickford, 28, and Douglas Fairbanks, 37, show up.

The New York *Times* reports that Harding's wife Florence, 59, who controls the queue of those who want inside, eats waffles for breakfast. Now everybody wants some.

Florence's own recipe, which cleverly features ingredients that had been rationed during the recent Great War, signals Harding's promised "return to normalcy." It's gone viral.

Harding's campaign is taking advantage of nationwide radio to keep his "America first" message in front of the public.

And the last three presidential candidates to use the "front porch" strategy? They all won.

For Florence Harding's waffle recipe see https://gshistory.com/tag/florence-harding/

❧ JUNE 28, 1920 ❧
CIVIC AUDITORIUM, SAN FRANCISCO, CALIFORNIA

For the opening of the Democratic National Convention, Prohibition appears to have been repealed. Each delegate is welcomed upon arrival in San Francisco by an attractive young woman proffering a bottle of illegal alcohol, courtesy of the mayor.

The front runner for the presidential nomination, at 2 to 1 odds, is Ohio Governor James. M. Cox, 50, who is still dodging questions about his divorce of nine years ago—just to clarify, he had been charged with cruelty, not infidelity.

Incumbent President Woodrow Wilson, 63, almost on his deathbed in Washington, DC, and former Secretary of State William Jennings Bryan, 60, whose political career *is* on its deathbed after three unsuccessful runs for high office, are each still unrealistically hopeful of getting the nomination.

Heywood Broun

Today, at the opening ceremony, as the New York *Tribune's* **Heywood Broun**, 31, reports:

> 66 A huge American flag fluttered from the ceiling…The flag was cheered. By and by the flag was raised and there nestling behind it was a large picture of President Wilson. It was not a very good picture, rather red-faced and staring and frightened, but it served as a symbol of the man in the White House, and the cheering burst out,

or if it didn't burst at any rate, it began…[The 21-minute pro-Wilson ovation was not] animated by sincerity."

In his keynote address, Democratic National Committee Chairman, twice-divorced Homer Cummings, 50, eulogizes Wilson and compares his tribulations to those of Christ on the cross. In **Broun's** opinion,

❝ It did not seem a great speech…although there were elements of excellence in the first hour and a half."

❧ JULY, 1920 ❧
CAPE COD, MASSACHUSETTS, AND
GREENWICH VILLAGE, NEW YORK CITY, NEW YORK

Edna St. Vincent Millay, 28, checking her new copy of the July issue of *Vanity Fair*, thinks, That sure paid off.

Edmund Wilson

At a Greenwich Village party back in April she had met Princeton grad Edmund "Bunny" Wilson, 25. He was immediately entranced by her bobbed red hair and impromptu poetry recital. She wasn't that interested—until she found out he was the new managing editor of *Vanity Fair.*

Shortly after, Edna had taken his virginity—well, he had offered it. Then she took off for Cape Cod for the summer, to stay in this borrowed cottage with her mother and sisters, without heat or electricity. She is happy banging out sonnets on her portable Corona typewriter.

Millay has had poems published before, in smaller magazines such as *Ainslee's* and *Current Opinion*, and her anti-war play *Aria da Capo* has been produced by the Provincetown Players.

But thanks to her suitor Bunny, she now has a poem in *Vanity Fair*, "Dead Music—An Elegy," accompanied by a plug for her play and a squib describing her as "one of the most distinctive personalities in modern American poetry." Thanks for that, Bunny.

Edna sees this as quite a step up, with her work nestled in between pieces by G. K. Chesterton, 46, Stephen Leacock, 50, and, oh, yes, John Peale Bishop, 28. He's coming to visit soon for a few days. But she plans to have him leave just before Bunny arrives.

❦

Second

Back in Greenwich Village, Egmont Arens, 32, owner of the Washington Square Bookshop on West Eighth Street, is setting out the July *Vanity Fair* along with the July-August issue of *The Little Review*.

Founded and edited by Margaret Anderson, 33, and Jane Heap, 36, for the past six years *The Little Review* has been publishing the most cutting-edge writers in America and abroad. Their foreign editor, ex-patriate American poet Ezra Pound, 34, has introduced them to the latest developments in literature from Europe.

Thanks to Pound, for the past two years *The Little Review* has been publishing excerpts from the latest work-in-progress, *Ulysses*, by the Irish novelist James Joyce, 38.

However, the authorities don't agree with Anderson and Heap's enthusiasm for contemporary literature. Last year, and again this January, issues of the magazine carrying the "Cyclops" chapter of *Ulysses* were seized and burned by the U. S. Post Office.

Since then, however, they have been left alone. March issue, no problem. April issue, no problem. Even the May-June issue, with the first two parts of Joyce's "Nausicaa" episode, had been published, sold and mailed with no interference.

This July-August issue contains the third part of "Nausicaa." Pound admits that, before sending the manuscript on to *The Little Review*, "I did myself dry [Stephen] Bloom's shirt," removing Joyce's reference to a semen stain.

We'll see if this issue will be left alone by the censors, thinks Arens. Fingers crossed.

❧ JULY 6, 1920 ❧
CIVIC AUDITORIUM, SAN FRANCISCO, CALIFORNIA

Almost over. Thank God. The endless Democratic National Convention is finally coming to a close. 9 days. 14 candidates. 44 ballots.

H. L. Mencken, 39, reporting for the Baltimore *Sun*, who had hated the smelly Chicago Coliseum where the Republicans held their convention last month, rhapsodizes about the Democrats' choice of venue, the Civic Auditorium:

> So spacious, so clean, so luxurious in its comforts and so beautiful in its decorations, that the assembled politicos felt like sailors turned loose in the most gorgeous bordellos of Paris."

Novelist, playwright and former full-time journalist Edna Ferber, 34 (but she only admits to 31), on special assignment for United Press, is as unimpressed with the Democratic delegates as she had been with those from the other party:

> It was, in its way, almost as saddening a sight as the Republican Convention had been…Once the opening prayer had piously died on the air, there broke out from two to a half dozen actual fist fights on the floor of the assemblage—battles that raged up and down the aisles until guards separated the contestants. The meeting droned on. Nothing seemed to be accomplished."

The New York *Tribune's* **Heywood Broun**, 31, however, gave the edge to the Republicans:

> They were able at Chicago to say nothing in just about one-tenth the number of words which the Democrats needed to say the same thing."

Every time a woman delegate was given the floor to nominate or second a candidate, the band played the ragtime hit, *Oh, You Beautiful Doll.*

By yesterday, everyone was so frustrated at the group's inability to decide on a candidate, the Missouri delegation cast a .50 vote for sportswriter Ring Lardner, 35, whose syndicated columns have been delighting the country. He says he will run on the same platform he used to not be elected mayor of Chicago:

❝ More Beer—Less Work.❞

Ring Lardner

Franklin D. Roosevelt and James M. Cox

Finally, at 1:43 am today, on the 44th ballot, Ohio Governor James M. Cox, 50, received enough votes to secure the nomination. When he is informed of this by the Associated Press telegraph wire three hours later in his Dayton office, he is stunned.

Now there is the matter of the running mate. Who to nominate for vice president?

Cox favors the new, young star of the show, Assistant Secretary of the Navy, and fifth cousin of the late Republican President Theodore Roosevelt, Franklin Delano Roosevelt, 38. As Cox says,

❝ His name is good, he's right geographically, and he is anti-Tammany [Hall]."

And FDR has been running around the convention making friends, wooing the rest of his New York state delegation by turning his rooms on the battleship *New York* into a Prohibition-violating reception.

That's good enough. The convention nominates Roosevelt by acclimation. Exhausted acclimation.

❧ JULY 11, 1920 ❧
34 RUE DU BOIS DE BOLOGNE, NEUILLY, PARIS

Sylvia Beach, 33, American ex-patriate bookshop owner, does not want to be at this dinner party.

Her partner, Adrienne Monnier, 28, owner of the Left Bank's other most popular bookshop, has been invited by the host, French poet Andre Spire, soon to turn 52, whom Adrienne knows well.

But Sylvia doesn't. Nevertheless, Adrienne is persuasive.

As Sylvia is planning a quick exit, Spire comes over and whispers to her,

" The Irish writer James Joyce is here."

That puts a different twist on it.

American poet Ezra Pound, 34, who is lounging in an armchair in a velvet jacket and open-collared blue shirt, has made sure that everyone in Paris knows that the amazing James Joyce, 38, is in town.

Beach has admired Joyce's work—from *Dubliners* to *A Portrait of the Artist as a Young Man*. Pound has spent the past month on a public relations campaign to line up ahead of time everything the Joyce family will need to live in Paris: first a hotel room, then a free apartment for three months, then a French translator for his work.

Beach chats with Nora Barnacle, 36, Joyce's partner for the last 16 years and mother of their two children. Nora is thrilled to be able to speak English with someone; for the past 10 years in Trieste, Italy, they've all been speaking Italian.

During a dinner of cold cuts and free-flowing wine, Joyce refuses any alcohol by turning his glass upside down. He's determined to not drink until 8 pm in the evenings.

Afterwards, Sylvia walks into the library and finds Joyce leaning against a bookcase; thin, a bit stooped. She cautiously approaches him, and, offering her hand, asks,

❝   Is this the great James Joyce?"

He limply shakes her hand saying, in his Dublin lilt, "James Joyce."

They talk about his family's move to Paris and she notices that his right eye looks odd, distorted by the thicker right lens of his glasses. He asks her,

❝   And what do you do in Paris, Miss Beach?"

He is enchanted by the name of her bookshop, Shakespeare & Company, and writes it down, along with the address, in his notebook held very close to his eyes. He tells her that he will visit soon.

Adrienne finds Sylvia and says that the guests are leaving. Beach shakes Joyce's hand again.

As she is walking out, Spire asks Sylvia if she has been bored. Beach replies,

❝   Bored? I have just met James Joyce!"

Thanks to Paris resident Gregory Grefenstette for help in pinpointing the location of this meeting.

❧ SUMMER, 1920 ☙

WINDSOR, VERMONT; WESTPORT, CONNECTICUT; AND NEW YORK CITY, NEW YORK

For the first time since he moved from the advertising department, at New York publisher Charles Scribner's Sons, up to the editorial department six years ago, Maxwell Perkins, 35, feels as though he is entitled to a vacation.

He is back in Windsor, Vermont, where he had spent most of his summers while growing up. It's peaceful. And quiet. And brings back good memories.

However, as usual, he worries about his writers. Particularly his new discovery **F. Scott Fitzgerald**, 23, whose debut novel, *This Side of Paradise*, is earning Perkins this welcome rest.

Max decides he'd better send **Scott** his summer address, just in case he needs to be in touch: "Maxwell Perkins, Windsor, Vermont."

Down south in Westport, Connecticut, **Scott** and his new bride, Zelda, about to turn 20, are spending most of their summer supporting the local bootlegger.

Working on short stories as well as his second novel, **Scott** flirts with Eugenia Bankhead, 19, sister of stage and screen actress Tallulah, 18, both schoolmates of Zelda.

The Fitzgeralds' rented house in Westport, Connecticut

Zelda fights back by chatting up *Smart Set* co-editor George Jean Nathan, 37.

So many drunk drivers are racing up and down the road between parties in Westport and New York, the local police have given up trying to stop them.

Riding through midtown Manhattan one day in a taxi, **Scott** starts sobbing. He knows that he has gotten everything he ever wanted. And life will never be this good again.

❧ JULY 22, 1920 ❧
MARION, OHIO

Three more weeks. In three more weeks the state legislatures of both Tennessee and North Carolina will meet and vote on whether to ratify the 19th Amendment to the Constitution giving women the right to vote in all elections in the country. A yes vote in either state will put the Amendment over the top, with 36 states ratifying.

Suffragettes in front of Warren G. Harding's front porch

More than 100 members of the National Woman's Party, dressed in white and carrying purple, green and white banners, are marching through the streets of Marion, Ohio, to the famed "front porch" of the Republican nominee for the presidency, Ohio Senator Warren G. Harding, 54. They know that this is as close to victory as they have ever been.

Alice Paul, 35, who helped draft the Amendment, points out to Harding that suffrage for women is the one plank in either party's platform that they can act on even before the election. All Harding has to do is put pressure on the Republican majority in Tennessee for them to vote aye.

Just yesterday Harding had sent a telegram to the most prominent suffragette, Carrie Chapman Catt, 61, co-founder of the National League of Women

Voters, pledging that, if the Tennessee Republicans asked for his opinion, he would "cordially recommend" that they vote yes.

Big of him.

In Marion, Ms. Paul says that, if Senator Harding "contents himself merely with 'earnestly hoping' and 'sincerely desiring,' how can he expect the country to take seriously the other planks in his platform?"

Louisine Havemeyer, 64, patron of the arts and suffragists, asks

   " " Is it fair that a woman should make the flag and only the men should wave it?...When President Abraham Lincoln wished to pass an amendment...did he say, 'I have done enough,' or...'I will urge,'...or 'Ladies, don't bother me, I have done all I could.' No....Isn't it time to end the struggle?"

Senator Harding is polite to the women.

Fifteen weeks until the general election.

✺ JULY 29, 1920 ✺
6 PLEASANT STREET, MONTGOMERY, ALABAMA

This whole adventure started a few weeks ago, back in Westport, Connecticut, when newlywed Zelda Sayre Fitzgerald, 19, was cranky over breakfast. She mused that the people of her home state of Alabama were

Marmon, c. 1920

❝ very beautiful and pleasant and happy, while up in Connecticut all the people ate bacon and eggs and toast, which made them very cross and bored and miserable—especially if they happened to have been brought up on biscuits…and I wish I could have some peaches anyhow."

She convinced her new husband, novelist **F. Scott Fitzgerald**, 23, that it was time for a road trip.

So they got in to the second-hand Marmon they had bought a few months ago, which Zelda had already "de-intestined" by running over a fire hydrant, and headed south, home to Montgomery.

Now here they are. They arrived yesterday. After more than a week and 1,200 miles, after

- Experiencing numerous breakdowns, including losing a tire, in the car they have christened "The Rolling Junk";

- Being robbed by highwaymen (almost);

- Running out of gasoline in the middle of nowhere;

- Getting a speeding ticket for going over 70 mph;

- Overcoming all the barriers to driving into Richmond, Virginia, to spend Zelda's 20th birthday touring the Confederate Museum in 94 degree weather;

- Navigating unpaved roads, bad signage and guidebooks, nasty weather and nastier locals;

- Being refused a room in a hotel because Zelda was wearing her custom-made white knickerbocker suit, matched to **Scott's**, including being told by some white trash in North Carolina,

66 It's a pity that a nice girl like you should be let to wear those clothes";

- Driving through every town in Alabama where Zelda could identify a different boyfriend she'd had; and

- Arriving here at Zelda's childhood home in Montgomery to find that her parents aren't home.

Still haven't had any peaches. Or biscuits.

Time to sell the Marmon. They'll take the train back north.

Montgomery Times' *"Society" column*

❧ AUGUST 2, 1920 ❧
ABBEY THEATRE, LOWER ABBEY STREET, DUBLIN

Opening night. Sara Allgood, 40, is ready. She has played the title character in *Cathleen ni Houlihan* many times, but not for a few years now. The play, billed as being by the poet **William Butler Yeats**, 55—but everyone knows that his fellow Abbey co-founder **Lady Augusta Gregory**, 68, wrote most of it—has become the Abbey's signature piece.

Premiered back in 1902, before the theatre even had this building on Abbey Street, the star then was **Yeats'** love, English-Irish activist Maud Gonne, now 53, and the play caused quite a stir for its nationalistic themes. Some critics said Gonne was just playing herself.

Sara Allgood

The theatre has staged *Cathleen* many times, including for its own opening night as the Abbey, during the Christmas holidays in 1904, when Sara played a smaller part.

The seven performances this week—including the Saturday matinee—are the first time it's been performed at the Abbey since St. Patrick's Day last year. On the infamous night when **Lady Gregory** herself stepped into the lead role when the scheduled actress was taken ill.

So no pressure there, Sara.

After this run, she jumps next week right in to the lead in the late **John Millington Synge's** masterpiece, *Riders to the Sea*. Just three performances for that gem, about a widow who loses all her sons to the sea. For a one-act, it's an emotional roller coaster.

Later in the month, she's scheduled to star in some of the smaller plays the Abbey is known for. She's looking forward to working again with one of their new stars, Barry Fitzgerald, 32, who had his breakthrough just last year in **Lady Gregory's** *The Dragon*.

A widow herself, having lost her husband to the Spanish flu two years ago, Sara is proud that she has been able to have a career as a full-time actress for the past 15 years.

❦ EARLY AUGUST, 1920 ❧
31 NASSAU STREET
NEW YORK CITY, NEW YORK

Margaret Anderson, 33, founder and publisher of the six-year-old magazine *The Little Review*, doesn't want to have to be here.

But her magazine needs money. Again. And this is one of the only ways she knows how to get it.

Margaret Anderson

The lawyer she is waiting to see, patron of the arts John Quinn, 50, has been a key source of her funding for the past few years. The magazine's foreign editor, American ex-patriate poet Ezra Pound, 34, had brought them together. The first time they met, three years ago, at Quinn's fashionable penthouse apartment, looking out over Central Park West, Anderson had been impressed. Quinn wanted to help bankroll the magazine, but also felt he could tell them how to run it. On an art collector-lawyer's budget. Not realistic for a semi-monthly publication produced out of the Greenwich Village apartment she shares with her partner, Jane Heap, 36, editor of *The Little Review.*

Quinn had pulled together some American investors and given Pound money to find and pay Europe's best poetry contributors for the magazine.

More recently, *The Little Review* has attracted the attention of the authorities, particularly the U. S. Post Office. Quinn had defended the first charge brought against them for publishing an allegedly obscene short story which was distributed through the mails. Now their serialization of *Ulysses*, the latest work by Pound's find, James Joyce, 38, the Irish writer living in Paris, has been under threat of confiscation. Quinn is going to defend them again, if needs be. Anderson hopes.

Now she needs more cash. She hadn't even bothered to phone Quinn to ask if she could come by his office. Anderson is wearing one of her best grey suits; her blonde hair is tucked under her little black hat; she's lost some weight; she's learned the way to smile at Quinn to make him think that she just might be interested in him. [She isn't.]

The Little Review is once again in danger of going under. Could Quinn go back to some of the original investors he'd rounded up and see if any is willing to provide more support? Being the first to publish Joyce's work in America is a real coup.

Quinn is tired of asking his friends for cash. He gives Anderson a check for $200 and sends her away. He's determined that this will be his last contribution to *The Little Review*. And regrets having given them this one.

✿ MID-AUGUST, 1920 ✿
NEAR THE HOTEL ELYSEE, RUE DE BEAUNE, PARIS

American poet, T. S. Eliot, 31, is finishing up a lovely meal with his traveling companion, English painter and writer, Wyndham Lewis, 37, and their newly met friend, Irish novelist James Joyce, 38.

James Joyce with his son, Giorgio, a few years before

Eliot and Lewis have come to visit Paris from London. Before leaving, another American ex-patriate poet, Ezra Pound, 34, had given them a package to bring to Joyce. So today they invited him to their hotel to get acquainted.

Earlier in the summer, Joyce had written to Pound, one of his many benefactors, describing the poverty his family was enduring—he had to wear second hand clothing and the too-large boots of his 15-year-old son, Giorgio.

Joyce wasn't surprised when Eliot got in touch, but was curious as to the package he had brought from Pound.

Giorgio had come with his father to meet the visitors. When Joyce opened the package from Pound and saw that it contained old brown shoes and used clothes, Joyce was clearly embarrassed. He told Giorgio to take the package home and tell his mother that Dad wouldn't be home for dinner. Giorgio clearly didn't want to go, and the two had a bit of fight, in Italian.

Eliot had invited Joyce to come with them to this nearby restaurant for dinner, but now the Irishman is insisting on paying the whole bill. And leaving a very big tip.

❧ AUGUST **16, 1920** ❧
WESTPORT, CONNECTICUT

❝ It's been a wild summer, thank God."

Zelda Fitzgerald, 20, is writing to a friend. Her husband, **F. Scott**, 23, has been spending long hours working on his second novel, *The Flight of the Rocket*. He has described it to his publisher, Charles Scribner, II ["Old C. S."], 65,

❝ How [the hero] and his beautiful young wife are wrecked on the shoals of dissipation is told in the story....I hope [it] won't disappoint the critics who liked my first one [*This Side of Paradise*]."

Zelda manages to drive into New York City fairly often, with and without her husband. And carry on a bit of an affair with *Smart Set* magazine co-editor, George Jean Nathan, 38, whose specialties are absinthe cocktails and married women.

Recently, Nathan had invited both **Fitzgeralds** to a midweek party at his West 44th Street apartment at the Royalton Hotel, so **Scott** could meet Nathan's fellow editor, H. L. Mencken, 39. The young novelist was thrilled to get to know one of his literary heroes, who rarely shows up at these midtown Manhattan parties. Nathan had managed to procure three cases of bootleg gin for the occasion.

Zelda is describing what she remembers of the party to her friend,

❝ I cut my *tail* on a broken bottle and can't possibly sit on the three stitches that are in it now—The bottle was bath salts—I was boiled—The place was a tub somewhere."

Zelda has no idea how she ended up in Nathan's tub, but she has been known to take impromptu baths at parties before.

A few weeks ago, **Scott** had written to his agent,

" I can't seem to stay solvent—but I think if you can advance me $500…I'll be able to survive the summer."

Smart Set *editors H. L. Mencken and George Jean Nathan*

❧ LATE AUGUST, 1920 ❧
OGUNQUIT, MAINE

Irish-American art collector and supporter of the arts John Quinn, 50, is finally able to relax.

Earlier this summer he had rented this cottage on the Maine coast, for his sister, Julia Quinn Anderson, in her mid-thirties [but not her damned husband!]; her daughter, Mary, 13; the French couple who serve as Quinn's house servants; and a professional nurse to care for Julia.

Julia is recuperating from a bout of illness, and Quinn had planned to stay with them up here for this whole month. But work in his busy Manhattan law firm had kept him in the city until just last week. He's hoping they can all stay here well in to September.

Before leaving for this vacation, Quinn had made a point of getting caught up on all his correspondence:

To English painter and writer Wyndham Lewis, 37, he wrote complaining about his disappointment with the Welsh painter Augustus John, 42:

❝ I responded for years to his calls for advance of money, and he promised me the first chance at his best work, but he constantly broke his word…So I finally broke with him."

To his friend, Irish poet **William Butler Yeats**, 55, he wrote,

❝ Much as I admire the work of modern French painters, they sometimes seem to me to carry their simplification, their abhorrence of a story, of a complete scene, too far and to go on too much for flowers and fruit and still-lifes and simplification of design that, seen by themselves, are satisfying, but they would become monotonous if seen in a large group of the same kind…Now I must write to…[Abbey Theatre director **Lady Augusta Gregory**, 68], to whom I regret to

say I have not written in
some months. I hope that
when writing to her…
you told her how busy and
overworked I have been."

To novelist Joseph Conrad, 62,
whose manuscripts Quinn has
been buying, he wrote praising
his latest work, and then added a
cautionary note:

Joseph Conrad

❝ …[I have] learned by
bitter experience what it is
to overwork and to drive
one's body more than it
can stand…[For the past
25 years, I have] worked
hard, had made some
money, and spent it or
given it away without thought…"

Now Quinn needs a rest. Here, with his only family.

My thanks to the Historical Society of Wells and Ogunquit for their help in researching this post.

❧ 8 AM, EST, AUGUST 26, 1920 ❧
WASHINGTON, DC

Alice Paul and suffragists celebrating

U.S. Secretary of State Bainbridge Colby, 50, certifies the ratification of the 19th Amendment by the Tennessee legislature eight days before, signing the Proclamation of the Women's Suffrage Amendment to the U. S. Constitution. Women's right to vote in all elections throughout the country goes into effect as law.

The suffragists who worked for more than 70 years to get the Amendment passed breathe a collective sigh of relief. They immediately turn their energies to getting an Equal Rights Amendment introduced in Congress.

For a brief history of how the amendment became law, see https://www. youtube.com/watch?v=TWX4H6sAgtY

For more in-depth context from Soledad O'Brien, see https://www.youtube. com/watch?v=YhgXsY4osvM

❦ SUMMER, 1920 ❦
LINDSEY HOUSE
100 CHEYNE WALK, CHELSEA, LONDON

Sir Hugh Lane

She is not going to give up. Playwright and co-founder of the Abbey Theatre, **Lady Augusta Gregory**, 68, is determined that the extensive art collection owned by her nephew, the late Sir Hugh Lane, only 39 when he went down on the RMS *Lusitania*, will go to the city of Dublin.

To show his anger at the Dublin City Corporation for making it so difficult for him to create a gallery to hold his collection, Lane had withdrawn his offer and changed his will to bequeath the art to the National Gallery in London.

However, just before he boarded the *Lusitania* in New York City, back in May of 1915, he had a change of heart and wrote out a codicil to the will, giving the paintings to Dublin. He carefully initialled each page, but neglected to have the document witnessed.

And so the battle wages on between Dublin and London. With **Augusta** in the middle.

She has enlisted the support of her fellow founder of the Abbey, poet and playwright **William Butler Yeats**, 55. A few years ago, **Willie** had written a poem, "To a Shade," chastising the Dublin newspaper owner who was leading the assault against this generous gift from a generous man:

> And insult heaped upon him for his pains,
> And for his open-handedness, disgrace;
> Your enemy, an old foul mouth, had set
> The pack upon him."

The critics point out that living conditions in Dublin tenements are appalling; why should money be spent for rich men's art?

In the poem **Yeats** counters by pointing out that art in a public gallery will give the Irish

> ...loftier thought,
> Sweeter emotion, working in their veins."

But by now, even **Yeats** is ready to give up the fight.

Lady Augusta Gregory

Not **Augusta**.

This summer, staying in Lane's London flat in Cheyne Walk, she is corresponding with anyone who can possibly help. In June alone she has written to Irish painters and sculptors who would want to have their work included in a Dublin gallery alongside the major French Impressionists Lane specialized in.

Lady Gregory has even written to blatant unionists like Sir Edward Henry Carson, 66, head of the Irish Unionist Party, hoping he could serve as a go-between. She has heard back from museum curators, aristocrats, trustees of the London National Gallery, and even the recent UK Chief Minister for Ireland Ian MacPherson, 40.

No progress.

Having just two years ago lost her only son, Robert, when he was shot down by friendly fire in Italy, age 36, **Augusta** is not ready to give up on the last wishes of her favorite nephew.

Not yet. Not ever.

❧ SEPTEMBER, 1920 ❧
57 WEST 57TH STREET
NEW YORK CITY, NEW YORK

To be honest, it's not great. The apartment that free-lance writer **Dorothy Parker**, 27, is planning to rent at the corner of Sixth Avenue and 57th Street on the Upper West Side, is not great.

But **Parker** feels that she and her husband, Eddie, also 27, a veteran of the Great War, really need a change.

Neysa McMein

Currently they are living farther uptown on 71st and West End Avenue. Eddie seems to have his morphine addiction under control, but still drinks. He has started back to work at Paine Webber, and she is selling lots of stories, articles and poems to magazines like *Life, The Saturday Evening Post, Ladies Home Journal.*

But the **Parkers** definitely need a change, and this could be it.

Dorothy has been looking around midtown and hasn't come up with any better alternatives. One place an agent had shown her was much too big. She told him,

❝ All I need is room enough to lay a hat and a few friends."

This dusty three-story building, right near the rattling, noisy Sixth Avenue El, has a tiny place available on the top floor.

The studios are designed for artists to use, not necessarily live in. One of the illustrators here is Neysa McMein, 32, whose apartment is used as a drinking hangout by many of their mutual friends, writers who lunch regularly at the Algonquin Hotel, right off Sixth Avenue on West 44th Street, a short walk away.

Another advantage is the Swiss Alps restaurant, on the ground floor of the building. They deliver.

So **Parker** is determined to sign a lease and move in with her seed-spilling canary, Onan, her not yet housebroken Scottish terrier, Woodrow Wilson, and her still traumatized husband.

If that doesn't save this marriage, nothing will.

❧ SEPTEMBER, 1920 ❧
PARIS

Almost 30,000 Americans are living permanently in Paris. And not everyone is thrilled with them. Even some of their fellow Americans. One had his letter to the editor published in the paper:

❝ Sir:

Couldn't you...help get a law passed requiring that muzzles be placed on all our American intellectual aristocrats before they are turned loose in the iniquitous regions of Montparnasse and the Cafe du Dome where they sit on the terrace from noon til midnight, soaking up various forms of alcoholic beverage and categorically condemning

America and all things American with the ignorant assurance of youth?... Among other things I heard them refer to our President as a 'cheap politician and an intellectual nonentity' and the Statue of Liberty as a 'monument to our Illustrious Death.'"

Soaking up alcoholic beverage at the Café du Dome

❧ MID-SEPTEMBER, 1920 ❧
BOSTON, MASSACHUSETTS

I rish-American lawyer and art collector, John Quinn, 50, and his family—sister Julia Quinn Anderson, in her mid-thirties; niece Mary, 13; two French household servants and a private nurse—are at the Boston South Station waiting for their train back to Quinn's home in New York City.

They have all just finished a lovely long holiday at a cottage in Ogunquit on the coast of Maine, courtesy of Quinn. John wasn't able to join them until just a few weeks ago. But he really appreciated relaxing at the resort. He hired a car and driver from Portsmouth, New Hampshire, to bring them here to Boston—well worth the cost, including $12 tip.

Boston South Station

Quinn notices that Boston is, as he later writes to a friend,

> " turned over to the Irish, who turned out…one hundred thousand strong to greet [Irish politician Eamon de Valera, 37]. I am told that 70% of the population of Boston is Irish…There is one spot on the earth where the Irish are on top."

De Valera, self-proclaimed President of Dáil Éireann, the Parliament of the new Irish Republic, addresses a crowd of 50,000 at Fenway Park near the end of his American tour, selling bonds to support his new government.

Nearby, two Italian immigrants, Nicola Sacco, 29, and Bartolomeo Vanzetti, 32, are indicted for a robbery and double murder at a shoe factory in Braintree, Massachusetts, last April.

For silent newsreel footage of de Valera's trip to Boston, see https://ifiplayer. ie/eamon-de-valera-in-boston/.

❧ MID-SEPTEMBER, 1920 ❧
MANHATTAN, NEW YORK CITY, NEW YORK

Alexander McKaig, 25, is enjoying a quiet evening in his apartment, when in through the door bursts his friend and former Princeton classmate, **F. Scott Fitzgerald**, about to turn 24, and his new bride, Zelda, 20. Fighting. As always.

Apparently, they had just jumped on a train to Manhattan when their most recent squabble brought them to the Westport, Connecticut, train station, near their current rented home. Zelda had almost been run over by a train while crossing the Saugatuck River railroad bridge.

Since the **Fitzgeralds** moved to Westport early in the summer, McKaig's impression is that they party and fight all the time. The most recent big blow out had been over Labor Day weekend.

Why all the drama? **Scott's** writing career appears to be going well. Based on the success of his first novel, *This Side of Paradise*, earlier this year, his publisher, Charles Scribner's Sons, brought out a collection of his short stories, *Flappers and Philosophers*, just last week.

The **Fitzgeralds** are always complaining about having no money. But Alex knows that an advance on the Scribner's royalties bought Zelda a new fur coat. And **Fitzgerald** has sold some of his stories to Hollywood movie studios for thousands of dollars.

What on earth are they always fighting about?!

After listening to Zelda yet again threaten to leave **Scott** for good, McKaig determines that he won't attend their next upcoming drunken party in Westport.

❧ SEPTEMBER, 1920 ❧
MONK'S HOUSE, EAST SUSSEX, ENGLAND

At their East Sussex home, Monk's House, **Virginia**, 38, and **Leonard Woolf**, 39, often welcome weekend guests.

This weekend, one of their star authors at their own Hogarth Press, American ex-patriate Thomas Stearns Eliot, about to turn 32, is coming for the first time.

T. S. Eliot

A few years ago, they were very impressed with Eliot's poem published by The Egoist Press. "The Love Song of J. Alfred Prufrock," and wrote asking if they could bring out a collection of his poetry. They published 200 copies of Tom's *Poems* last year, selling for 2 shillings, 6 pence each. When **Leonard** closed out the account last month, they had paid Tom 4 pounds, 17 shillings, 4 pence, and made a nice profit for themselves of 9 pounds, 6 shillings, 10 ½ pence. The **Woolfs** feel that this is an indication, after five years in business, that the Hogarth Press is making good progress toward becoming a "real" publisher.

Ovid Press, also based in London, has published a private edition of Eliot's *Ara Vus Prec*—vellum paper, Moroccan leather binding, gold lettering—which has almost all the same poems in it.

From the beginning, **Virginia** and **Leonard** have been clear that they are most interested in what the author has to say. The Hogarth Press books definitely look good, and they sometimes experiment with typography, but they are meant to be read more than just looked at.

The risk the **Woolfs** took on publishing the unknown Eliot has paid off for him as well—the major American publisher Alfred A. Knopf brought out a U. S. version of his *Poems* earlier this year.

Tom still has a day job at a bank, but some of his friends and fans are talking about putting together a fund to support him and his work.

Virginia is mostly looking forward to talking to Tom over tea about his writing. She feels that sometimes his words need just a bit more explanation.

❧ SEPTEMBER **28, 1920** ❧
CHICAGO, ILLINOIS

Joe Jackson, 33, now former outfielder for the Chicago White Sox, is back in his hotel room after testifying to a Cook County grand jury about whether he was involved in fixing last year's World Series, played against the Cincinnati Reds. Which the White Sox lost, to everyone's surprise. Except the bookies.

Jackson had been eager to tell the jury that he had taken the $5,000 offered to him by another teammate to throw three games, but he hadn't earned it. Joe testified that throughout all the Series games he had "batted to win, fielded to win, and run the bases to win." He had played better than almost any ball player ever.

Shoeless Joe Jackson

In addition, he'd been promised *$20,000!*

After his testimony, a remorseful Jackson repeatedly told the crush of reporters waiting outside the courthouse,

❝ All I got was the $5000...handed me in a dirty envelope. I never got the other $15,000. I told that to [the judge]. He said he didn't care what I got...I don't think the judge likes me. I never got the $15,000 that was coming to me."

The next day, Joe is astounded to read in the Chicago *Daily News* this account of what happened when he came out of the Cook County Courthouse:

" When Jackson left the criminal court building…he found several
hundred youngsters, aged from six to 16, waiting for a glimpse of
their idol. One child stepped up to the outfielder, and, grabbing his
coat sleeve, said: 'It ain't true, is it, Joe?' 'Yes, kid, I'm afraid it is,'
Jackson replied. The boys opened a path for the ball player and stood
in silence until he passed out of sight. 'Well, I'd never have thought
it,' sighed the lad."

What youngsters?! When the hell had that happened?! Joe wonders.

❧ OCTOBER, 1920 ❧
HOGARTH HOUSE, RICHMOND, LONDON

The scheme seems to be working. **Leonard Woolf**, 39, co-founder and owner with his wife **Virginia**, 38, of the five-year-old Hogarth Press, is poring over the company accounts. It appears the subscription scheme the **Woolfs** implemented almost a year and a half ago is working.

The two-tiered system was set up so "A" list subscribers pay £1 for a commitment to buy all the titles printed by Hogarth in a given year. Last year there were five, including T. S. Eliot's *Poems*.

"B" list subscribers pay nothing up front, but are notified early of new releases and can choose which they want to buy.

So far, Hogarth has 34 people on the "A" list and 15 on the "B" list.

Hogarth Press logo, designed by Virginia's sister, Vanessa Bell

Truth be told, almost all of the subscribers are the **Woolfs'** friends and family. Some are well-known writers among their Bloomsbury Group friends—essayist **Lytton Strachey**, 40, economist **John Maynard Keynes**, 37. Some are established authors in their own right—H. G. Wells, 54, whose *War of the Worlds* had been a big hit two decades ago, and Rebecca West, 27, already known for her novel about the Great War, *The Return of the Soldier*, and a biography of late American writer Henry James.

Hiring an assistant to help out two or three days a week, Ralph Partridge, 26—chosen on **Lytton's** recommendation—also seems to have been a good move. The **Woolfs** have promised to pay him £100 for the year, as well as half of their net profits. Last year Hogarth Press netted a respectable 13 pounds, 14 shillings and 2 pence. Young Ralph is working on the press in their home, setting type, etc., as well as serving as **Leonard's** secretary. So **Virginia** and **Leonard** feel that the expense will pay off.

Ralph has been living out in the country with **Lytton** and their mutual love, painter Dora Carrington, 27. Now that he has a job, Ralph has convinced Carrington to move into a Bloomsbury Gordon Square townhouse with him. He hopes by the end of the year to finally convince her to marry him. **Lytton** is encouraging this.

❧ OCTOBER, 1920 ❧
100 EAST CHICAGO STREET, CHICAGO, ILLINOIS

This'll be another great party. Free-lance journalist **Ernest Hemingway**, 21, and his roommate are headed to their friends' apartment—which they call "The Domicile"—for one of their regular Sunday parties.

Ernest has had a really good year. It began with him entertaining a local women's group with stories of his experiences and injuries in the Great War [he embellished them just a little]. He was so impressive that a wealthy couple hired him to live in their Toronto, Canada, mansion as a companion to their disabled teenaged son.

Ernest Hemingway

The kid was a bore. But through the family's connections, **Ernie** managed to get a position writing for the Toronto *Star Weekly* magazine. And after some unsigned pieces of his were published, he finally got a byline! In "Taking a Chance for a Free Shave" by **Ernest M. Hemingway** he told the tale of his trip to a local barber college.

Even when he went for his usual trout fishing trip up in Michigan this past spring, he was still able to have bylined pieces most weeks in both the *Star* and the Chicago *Tribune*. His parents weren't happy that **Ernest** had no plans, and after a raucous beach party at the family lake cottage last summer—the neighbors complained—his mother had thrown him out, hand delivering to him a lengthy, nasty letter which said in part,

" Stop trading your handsome face to fool little gullible girls and neglecting your duties to God and your Saviour…Do not come back until your tongue has learned not to insult and shame your mother."

Hadley Richardson

A bit harsh.

Soon after, **Hemingway** went out one night with his last $6 in his pocket to a high class, although illegal, gambling house in Charlevoix, Michigan, and walked out at 2 am with $59 from the roulette tables. That was enough to keep him going without having to ask his parents for money. **Ernie** packed up some of his things from home and moved here to Chicago with a friend from his days when he served in the Red Cross ambulance corps in Italy during the War.

Hemingway is getting by with free-lance work; although his journalism is selling better than the short stories he's been submitting.

As he walks into the apartment of his friend, advertising guy Y. Kenley Smith, 32, **Ernest** sees a tall, auburn-haired woman across the room.

After striking up a conversation with Hadley Richardson, 28 [he lies to her about his age], he learns that she lives in St. Louis, plays the piano, and is here for a few weeks visiting Kenley's sister. She reminds him a bit of the nurse who took care of him when he was injured in Italy, who was also a bit older than he was. But, despite a year at Bryn Mawr College, and a trip to Paris, "Hash" as her friends call her, seems a bit younger than her age.

As he leaves the party, **Ernest** knows that he really wants to go back to live in Europe. And he knows that he is going to marry Hadley Richardson.

❧ OCTOBER, 1920 ❧
GRADUATE SCHOOL FOR ARTS AND SCIENCES
HARVARD UNIVERSITY, CAMBRIDGE, MASSACHUSETTS

Thomas Wolfe, just turned 20, recently graduated with a BA in English from the University of North Carolina, can't believe he is finally here at Harvard.

Wolfe's parents agreed to an advance on his inheritance so that he could enrol here to study playwriting. His mother's boarding house back home in Asheville, North Carolina, has done well over the years, but it is still a bit of a financial stretch for them to send him here.

Tom was set on Harvard so that he could study playwriting with the legendary Professor George Pierce Baker, 54. His English

THOMAS CLAYTON WOLFE
ASHEVILLE, N. C.
Age, 19; Weight, 178; Height, 6 feet 3 inches

Thomas Wolfe at University of North Carolina

47 class is world renowned as a training ground for successful playwrights, and Baker founded the university's Drama Club over a decade ago. Wolfe is hopeful that his play *The Mountains*, about his hometown, may be performed by Baker's "47 Workshop" next year; quite an honor.

Tom has already gotten good feedback from both Baker and his all-male classmates, as he writes home to his mother:

     "   Prof. Baker read the prolog of my play...to the class a week ago. To my great joy he pronounced it the best prolog ever written here. The class, harshly critical as they usually are, were unanimous in praising it. This circumstance bewilders as well as pleases me. I am acutely no judge of my own work...The work over which I expend the most labor and care will fail to impress while other work, which I have written swiftly, almost without revision will score."

❧ OCTOBER, 1920 ❧
No. 15 Ely Place, Dublin

Irish poet and playwright **William Butler Yeats**, 55, is recovering from a hemorrhage in the consulting rooms of his long-time friend, Dr. Oliver St. John Gogarty, 42, who has just removed his tonsils.

Yeats and his wife, Georgie, 28, have been living in Oxford, England, since returning from his long American lecture tour. When **Willie's** tonsils first flared up, he had tried to go to London to see a specialist. But he got lost.

After Georgie checked with her star charts, they decided the wasted trip to London was a bad omen. So they both came over here to Dublin to have Gogarty take care of him.

All that **Yeats** remembers at this point is Gogarty putting him under with ether, yapping away about literature. And when he awoke, bleeding, the good doctor took up his monologue exactly where he had broken off.

No. 15 Ely Place

By this point, lying in recovery, **Yeats** is feeling that his own end might be near, and starts to compose his dying speech. He is also thinking of tweaking his bedclothes to give the nurses a thrill.

❧ OCTOBER 21, 1920 ❧
GREENWICH VILLAGE, NEW YORK CITY, NEW YORK;
AND RUE DE L'ASSOMPTION, PARIS

John Quinn, 50, attorney, art collector, and supporter of the arts and artists, doesn't want to have to be here.

But *The Little Review* magazine needs him. Again.

Here in Jefferson Market Police Court for the preliminary hearing into their obscenity trial, Quinn has asked *The Little Review's* founder and publisher, Margaret Anderson, 33, and her editor, Jane Heap, 37, to sit away from him.

It's bad enough that he has to be here, pro bono, when he should be in Washington, DC, preparing for the corporate case he is set to argue before the U. S. Supreme Court. For a big fee.

Quinn only rushed over here because, after he stopped in his midtown law office following an important corporate meeting in the Bronx, the junior lawyer he had assigned to *The Little Review* case had called to say it would be best if Quinn were present in court. The magistrate, Judge Joseph E. Corrigan, 44, is not a fan of the New York Society for the Suppression of Vice [NYSSV] which brought the complaint. And he is an old friend of Quinn's from their involvement in Irish-American groups in the city.

So Quinn took the Sixth Avenue El down here to sit, in his three-piece suit with his gold watch chain spread across his vest, amidst the "immigrants, Negroes, Italians, and Lesbians," as he later describes them, waiting for Corrigan to finish privately reading the passage in question, the "Nausicaa" episode of *Ulysses*, by the genius—as far as Quinn is concerned—Irish novelist James Joyce, 38, published in the July-August issue of *The Little Review.*

Previous issues of the magazine with other *Ulysses* excerpts had been confiscated by the U. S. Post Office. But this is the first time a warrant has been served for the arrest of Anderson, Heap and even bookstore owners

Jefferson Market Courthouse by the Sixth Avenue Elevated

who sold the magazine. Quinn managed to at least get charges against the book sellers dismissed and delay the preliminary hearing until now.

As Quinn understands it, some uptight conservative businessman had found a copy of this issue of *Little Review* with his teenage daughter's magazines—and read it. He was appalled by Gerty MacDowell flashing her knickers, and wrote a nasty letter to the New York City District Attorney asking how this smut could be kept out of the hands of unsuspecting readers—the magazine had been mailed unsolicited to his daughter!

The DA knew that there is a way—the NYSSV, directed by John Sumner, 44, whose mission is to rid New York of filth.

Quinn had taken Sumner to lunch last week, hoping to get all the charges dismissed. He gave the NYSSV director a copy of a glowing review of Joyce's work from the *Dial* magazine, and admitted that some of that language should not have been in a magazine. Quinn assured Sumner that he would stop Joyce from publishing his work-in-progress in *The Little Review*. Quinn has been urging Joyce to agree to private publication of a high-quality book version of *Ulysses*, and he's close to getting a publisher, Ben Huebsch, 44, to agree.

Sumner doesn't believe Quinn can get Joyce to withdraw the rights from the magazine. And he wants the smut eliminated.

Sumner's deposition only has to say that the material is "obscene, lewd, lascivious, filthy, indecent and disgusting." The law says that to quote passages would just repeat the offense.

But Judge Corrigan is not willing to take Sumner's word for it. So he has halted today's proceedings to retire to his chambers and read the relevant 16 pages of the issue himself.

When he comes back into court, he shoots a bit of a smile towards his friend, Quinn. He says that one passage "where the man went off in his pants [is definitely] smutty, filthy."

Then the judge orders Anderson and Heap held for trial, postponed until February. Quinn asks that they be released to his custody—a technicality, as he intends to spend no more time with them than professionally required. His junior lawyer pays their $25 bail—each—and they are all free to go.

The Little Review is thrilled. Anderson defiantly tells the judge that this trial "would be the making of *The Little Review*."

Quinn doesn't give a damn about the magazine or the women. He wishes they would go back to the stockyards of Chicago where they started. He feels work like Joyce's should be kept out of publications sent through the mail, where any teenager can see them. Quinn believes that literature belongs in books.

Now Quinn is looking forward to a week's hiking trip in the Catskills. He's bought new light woollen socks and rubber-soled shoes for the occasion.

At 5 rue l'Assomption James Joyce sits at the desk in his family's cramped three-room apartment trying to finish the "Circe" section of his novel.

5 rue l'Assomption

He's been working on *Ulysses* for six years, and on this part for six months. Joyce described his current state to a friend as "working like a galley-slave, an ass, a brute."

Joyce is aware that the sections he has sent to *The Little Review*, via their foreign editor, American poet living in London, Ezra Pound, about to turn 35, have been published. And confiscated. And in some cases burned.

He hasn't heard much more about it. The magazine's attorney, Quinn, says that Joyce would be better off pulling out of the publication and publishing an expensive privately printed book version. The legal controversy could even increase book sales! But Joyce doesn't want to lose his *Little Review* audience.

And he has to finish writing the book first. Joyce just wants to keep working.

❧ FALL, 1920 ❧
HARLEM, NEW YORK CITY, NEW YORK

Paul Robeson, 22, has a decision to make. Having graduated from Rutgers College last year, Robeson is now studying law here at Columbia University. Throughout his college years he has appeared in plays and done some singing at special events.

Now an opportunity has come up for a major role in a play by poet Ridgely Torrence, 47, the poetry editor of *The New Republic*, who is developing a reputation for writing plays about African-Americans rebelling against society. It's a good role—the title character in *Simon the Cyrenian*, to be performed at the Harlem YWCA.

Paul Robeson in his Rutgers College football uniform

Robeson is doing well at Columbia. Much better since he transferred here from New York University's Law School earlier this year, after just one semester. He feels more comfortable living and studying up here in Harlem than he did down in Greenwich Village.

The only snag has been that he has just spent several weeks in New York Presbyterian Hospital recovering from a football injury. The good news is—that's where he got to know Eslanda Goode, 24, the head chemist in the Surgical Pathology department.

They had run into each other in Harlem before, during summer school and at parties. But it was after his recent hospital stay that they began to date.

Goode is keen on Paul performing more. He enjoys his singing engagements, but thinks of that as a hobby. Essie really wants him to get into acting. She is encouraging Paul to take this part in Torrence's play.

Robeson figures he'll say yes just so she'll quit nagging him about it.

Eslanda Goode

❧ OCTOBER 29, 1920 ❧
COOK COUNTY COURTHOUSE, CHICAGO, ILLINOIS

Shoeless Joe Jackson and Assistant State Attorney Hartley Replogle

The Cook County grand jury announce their indictments of eight former White Sox players, including "Shoeless" Joe Jackson, 34, and five professional athletes turned gamblers, on several counts of "conspiracy to obtain money by false pretenses and/or a confidence game" for throwing the 1919 World Series.

Illinois Assistant State Attorney Hartley Replogle, 40, is confident that his office's handling of the "Black Sox" scandal will help in the upcoming November election.

✥ NOVEMBER 2, 1920 ✥
AMERICA

Westinghouse-owned KDKA-AM in Pittsburgh, Pennsylvania, the first public commercial radio station in the U.S., is on air for the first time, broadcasting the results of the presidential election. The small percentage of the population in the eastern United States who own radio sets can hear the announcers read results right off the ticker tapes as they come in.

And it's also the first national election when women can vote. More voters than ever before— looks as though it will be a more than 40% increase over 1916— are creating a Republican landslide that is spilling into local elections as well.

KDKA logo

Republican candidate Ohio Senator Warren G. Harding is about to be the first sitting senator and first Baptist elected president—on his 55th birthday.

More voters also mean more votes for the Socialist candidate, Eugene V. Debs, just about to turn 65, although he is currently serving time in federal prison on charges of sedition. If he gets the predicted almost 1 million votes, it will still be a smaller percentage than the record 6% he got when he ran in 1912.

The first lady-to-be, Florence Harding, 60, tells a friend,

❝ I don't feel any too confident, I can tell you. I haven't any doubt about him, but I'm not so sure of myself."

In Cook County, Illinois, the Assistant State Attorney, Hartley Replogle, 40, is about to be swept out in the Republican tide, and his whole team, working on prosecuting the Black Sox World Series scandal, will soon be replaced.

To see the centenary celebrations of KDKA's historic first broadcast, including a re-enactment of the Harding election results broadcast from a replica of the original studio, see https://duq.edu/celebrating-100-years-of-radio

❧ NOVEMBER, 1920 ❧
THE DIAL, CHICAGO, ILLINOIS,
AND *THE NATION*, LONDON, ENGLAND

Irish poet and playwright **William Butler Yeats**, 55, is pleased that this month his poem, "The Second Coming," is appearing in both the American magazine, *The Dial*, as well as *The Nation* in England.

Yeats wrote the poem back in January of last year, just a few months after the end of The Great War, during a frightening personal time for him. His young

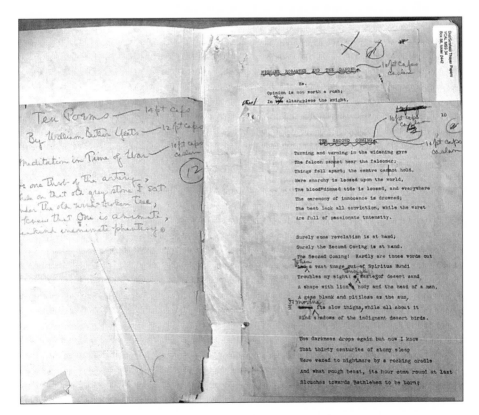

Typescript of "The Second Coming"

pregnant wife, Georgie, now 28, was hit hard by the Spanish influenza. Thankfully, she recovered and gave birth to their beautiful daughter, Anne, the following month.

𝄆 **The Second Coming**
By **W. B. Yeats**

"Turning and turning in the widening gyre
The falcon cannot hear the falconer;
Things fall apart; the centre cannot hold;
Mere anarchy is loosed upon the world,
The blood-dimmed tide is loosed, and everywhere
The ceremony of innocence is drowned;
The best lack all conviction, while the worst
Are full of passionate intensity.

Surely some revelation is at hand;
Surely the Second Coming is at hand.
The Second Coming! Hardly are those words out
When a vast image out of *Spiritus Mundi*
Troubles my sight: somewhere in sands of the desert
A shape with lion body and the head of a man,
A gaze blank and pitiless as the sun,
Is moving its slow thighs, while all about it
Reel shadows of the indignant desert birds.
The darkness drops again; but now I know
That twenty centuries of stony sleep
Were vexed to nightmare by a rocking cradle,
And what rough beast, its hour come round at last,
Slouches towards Bethlehem to be born?"

To hear a reading of "The Second Coming" see https://www. poetryfoundation.org/poems/43290/the-second-coming

❧ ARMISTICE DAY ❧
NOVEMBER 11, 1920
WESTMINSTER ABBEY, LONDON;
AND ARC DE TRIOMPHE, PARIS

Exactly two years after the Armistice which ended what H. G. Wells, now 54, has called "The War That Will End War," a ceremony is being held at Westminster Abbey to bury the remains of "A British Warrior who fell in the

The first ceremony for the interment of a British Unknown Warrior

Great War 1914–1918 for King and Country." This soldier has been chosen from among six exhumed from six different battlefields in France.

Rev. David Railton, 36, former British Army chaplain and now vicar of St. John the Baptist Church in Margate, had first thought of the idea when, during the war, he saw a makeshift cross over a grave that said, "An unknown British soldier." He proposed the monument just a few months ago in a letter to the government.

✂◦✄

Simultaneously, less than 300 miles south, a similar ceremony is being held beneath the Arc de Triomphe, where *La tombe du Soldat inconnu* is being consecrated. A French Army veteran has chosen one out of eight coffins containing remains of unknown French soldiers.

Last year, France's parliament voted into law the idea for such a tomb, proposed during the war by an officer of *Le Souvenir français*, France's war memorials body.

Ceremony consecrating La tombe du Soldat inconnu

❧ NOVEMBER, 1920 ❧
WEST 12TH STREET
NEW YORK CITY, NEW YORK

P oet Edna St. Vincent Millay, 28, is quite pleased with herself. When she came back to Manhattan after spending this summer in Cape Cod with her mother, sisters, and various visitors, she discovered that she had become famous.

Millay had won a $100 prize for a poem [and spent it all on clothes]. Her poetry collection, *A Few Figs from Thistles*, is in all the bookstores' windows.

And this month, one of her beaus, Edmund "Bunny" Wilson, 25, has given her poetry a whole page in *Vanity Fair*, where he is managing editor, calling her "the Most Distinguished American poet of the Younger Generation." In the issue she is squeezed between "The Anarchists of Taste" by Wilson and "The Art of Living as a Feminine Institution" by another *Vanity Fair* editor, John Peale Bishop, 28. Cozy.

My candle burns at both ends;
It will not last the night;
But ah, my foes,
and oh, my friends-
It gives a lovely light.

Edna St. Vincent Millay

"First Fig" from A Few Figs from Thistles

As she had indeed been squeezed between the two on her daybed in this apartment just recently. Edna insisted on assigning John her upper half, and Bunny the lower. He agreed that he had the "better share."

However, ironically, after having recently lent a birth control manual to her sister's boyfriend, Edna now thinks she might be pregnant.

❦ NOVEMBER 24, 1920 ❦
31 NASSAU STREET, NEW YORK CITY, NEW YORK;
AND RUE DE L'UNIVERSITE, PARIS

In his Manhattan law offices, John Quinn, 50, is stumped by the telegram he received yesterday from Irish novelist James Joyce, 38, in Paris.

POSTAL TELEGRAPH COMMERCIAL CABLES

TELEGRAM

The Postal Telegraph-Cable Company (Incorporated) transmits and delivers this message subject to the terms and conditions printed on the back of this blank.

COUNTER NUMBER.	TIME FILED.	CHECK.
	M.	

Send the following message, without repeating, subject to the terms and conditions printed on the back hereof, which are hereby agreed to.

SCOTTS TETTOJA MOIEDURA GEIZLSUND. JOYCE

Cable from James Joyce

Quinn sent his law clerk out to find some kind of code manual they could use to decipher it, and they have come up with:

> You will be receiving a letter upon this subject in a few days giving information and my views pretty fully. I think a little delay will not be disadvantageous."

Quinn's a bit disappointed, to say the least. He had written an *urgent* letter to Joyce almost a month ago, firmly telling him to contact *The Little Review* magazine and withdraw the rights to serialize his work in progress, *Ulysses*.

In the past year or so, the issues of the magazine carrying chapters of *Ulysses* have been seized, burnt, and now confiscated by the New York district attorney in preparation for an upcoming trial on grounds of obscenity.

Quinn is convinced that the DA might drop the charges if *Ulysses* is withdrawn from the magazine. He cables Joyce that he wants legal custody of the manuscript before an upcoming meeting he has arranged with publisher Ben Huebsch, 44, who four years ago published the American editions of Joyce's *Dubliners* and *A Portrait of the Artist as a Young Man*. Quinn is sure that Huebsch will publish the full novel in a privately printed edition, which would be immune from proscution.

❧❧❧

In his freezing cold Paris hotel room, with a shawl wrapped around his head for warmth, Joyce responds by letter to Quinn's entreaties.

He points out that he has been working on *Ulysses* for six years now, at 20 different addresses, this most recent being the coldest. Having heard very little about the recent court case, Joyce tells Quinn that he has assumed that *The Little Review* is no longer being published—there's been no issue since the one in July-August which was confiscated—and so there is no need for him to withdraw the rights.

In previous letters, Joyce had reminded Quinn that Huebsch had talked to him about publishing *Ulysses* before, and actually threatened to bring out a pirated edition in the States if Joyce had his novel published in Europe. Joyce doesn't think the manuscript's current legal troubles will put Mr. Huebsch off from publishing the full book.

Now he just wants to get back to writing. Joyce is planning to finish the novel next year and then take a whole year off. Right now he is on the ninth draft of the "Circe" episode.

❧ END OF NOVEMBER, 1920 ❧
1230 NORTH STATE STREET, CHICAGO, ILLINOIS

On Sunday, the following ad appeared in the "Wanted—Male Help" section of the Chicago *Sunday Tribune*:

❝ ADVERTISING WRITER
EXPERIENCE NOT NECESSARY

Prominent Chicago advertising agency offers unusual opportunity to men capable of expressing themselves clearly and entertainingly in writing. A real opportunity to enter the advertising profession and be promoted as rapidly as ability warrants. State age, education, experience, if any, whether married or single, what you have been earning and, in fact, anything or everything which will give us a correct line on you. All communications considered strictly confidential. Address C122 Tribune."

Ernest Hemingway, 21, composes this response:

❝ No attempt will be made to write a trick letter in an effort to plunge you into such a paroxysm of laughter that you will weakly push over to me the position advertised in Sunday's *Tribune*.

You would probably rather have what facts there are and judge the quality of the writing from published signed articles that I can bring you.

I am twenty-four years old, have been a reporter on the Kansas City *Star* and a feature writer for the Toronto *Star*, and the Toronto *Sunday World.*

Am chronically unmarried.

War records are a drug on the market of course but to explain my lack of a job during 1918—served with the Italian Army because of inability to pass the U. S. physical exams. Was wounded July 8 on the Piave River—decorated twice and commissioned. Not that it makes any difference.

At present I am doing feature stuff at a cent and a half a word and they want five columns a week. Sunday stuff mostly.

I am very anxious to get out of the newspaper business and into the copy writing end of advertising. If you desire I can bring clippings of my work on the Toronto *Star* and Toronto *Sunday World* and you can judge the quality of the writing from them. I can also furnish whatever business and character references you wish.

Front page of the Chicago Sunday Tribune, *November 28, 1920*

Hoping that I have in a measure overcome your sales resistance—

very sincerely

1230 N. State Street
Chicago Illinois"

❧ DECEMBER, 1920 ❧
GREENWICH VILLAGE, NEW YORK CITY, NEW YORK

Robert McAlmon

Robert McAlmon, 25, met Dr. William Carlos Williams, 37, at a lower East Side party shortly after re-locating here to New York from Chicago earlier this year. They are both having some of their poetry accepted in small magazines, but have decided that the best way to get published is to start their own.

They have just finished producing their first issue of *Contact*. Mimeographed on paper donated by Bill's father-in-law; filled with typos; with no table of contents or advertising. They've lined up about 200 subscribers to provide some income. Dr. Williams, of course, is still earning money in his medical practice during the day and working on the publication in the evenings.

McAlmon, on the other hand, has been scraping along doing some nude modelling for art classes at nearby Cooper Union.

Their manifesto in this first issue states,

❝ We are here because of our faith in the existence of native artists who are capable of having, comprehending and recording extraordinary experience…We are interested in the writings of such individuals as are capable of putting a sense of contact, and of definite personal realization into their work."

Contact includes the first bibliography of all the "little mags" that have been published in the States in the new century.

Williams and **McAlmon** feel strongly that American literature needs a publication such as *Contact,* as there are plenty of opportunities for writers from abroad, like *The Little Review.*

❧ DECEMBER, 1920 ❧
1230 NORTH STATE STREET, CHICAGO, ILLINOIS

Ernest Hemingway, 21, is settling in to his new job as editor—and primary writer—of *Cooperative Commonwealth*, the house organ of the Cooperative Society of America.

Ernie isn't quite sure how the Society operates, but "cooperative" sounds good enough to him. So does $40 a week.

Although the job gets heavy around deadline, the rest of the time he can make his own schedule. Most days **Hemingway** comes home here for lunch and gets a lot of the copy writing done for the 100-page issue in the afternoon.

Sherwood Anderson

Today at lunch he has received a picture card from the St. Louis woman he met at a party a few months ago, Hadley Richardson, inscribed on the back, "Most awfully lovingly, **Ernestonio** from your Hash. December, 1920."

Ernest and his roommates, who work in advertising, all have ambitions to become more than just hired hacks. Among their role models are "real" writers who are still doing some advertising copy to keep afloat.

For example, **Sherwood Anderson**, 44, had a huge hit last year with his first novel, *Winesburg, Ohio*, which scandalized middle America—including **Ernest's** parents—with its frank discussions of sex. **Anderson** has been contributing to *Cooperative Commonwealth*, and still does some work for his former ad agency, Critchfield.

Ernie and his fellow writers buy copies of radical magazines like *The Little Review* at their local bookstores, and know that their current writing for hire is a necessary evil until some major publisher recognizes their true talents for writing fiction.

❧ DECEMBER 12, 1920 ❧
5 BOULEVARD RASPAIL
QUARTIER SAINT GERMAIN, PARIS

Irish novelist James Joyce, 38, and his family are pleased to finally be settling in to this posh apartment near Saint Sulpice.

One of their benefactors, ex-patriate poet Ezra Pound, 35, has helped the Joyces with everything since they moved here to Paris in the summer, including getting a friend to let them rent this fabulous place for only £300 for six months.

5 boulevard Raspail, Quartier Saint Germain, Paris

Today he is writing to Ezra, in London, to tell him how sick and cold he had been in the previous, dark hotel. He was suffering from iritis again, and it was so cold there, he had to wrap a blanket around his shoulders and a shawl around his head to work on his novel, *Ulysses*, expanding the section to be known as "Circe."

Since he moved his family up to this posh flat, he wrote to another friend,

    ❝ By the way, is it not extraordinary the way I enter a city barefoot and end up in a luxurious flat?"

❧ DECEMBER, 1920 ❧
GREENWICH VILLAGE
NEW YORK CITY, NEW YORK

The most recent issue of *The Little Review*—the September-December number—is finally on the desk of the publisher Margaret Anderson, 34.

Anderson is proud of the mix of the 90 pages of content: Work by emerging American talents such as Djuna Barnes, 28 Ben Hecht, 27, **Robert McAlmon**, 25, **Man Ray**, 30. Five pages of poems by the German avant-garde artist Else von Freytag-Loringhoven, 46. Many reviews and discussions of recent literature.

The jewel in the crown is the 11-page excerpt from Episode XIV of *Ulysses*, the ongoing novel by Irishman James Joyce, 38, living in Paris and submitting his work via *The Little Review's* foreign editor, Ezra Pound, 35, in London.

But there are two long essays in the front of the magazine of which Anderson is particularly proud: The lead article, "The Art of Law," by Jane Heap, 37, the magazine's editor and Anderson's partner; and her own piece defending their publication of sections of *Ulysses*. Anderson remembers that she was so exasperated when she was finishing the essay, she titled it "An Obvious Statement (for the millionth time)."

Margaret Anderson and Jane Heap

Jane is much better at being witty and pithy. She makes the points that the courts are not qualified to judge works of art, and that the real problem is that sex education is almost unheard of for the "young girls" who are supposedly being protected by the censors, the New York Society for the Suppression of Vice [NYSSV].

In her own piece, Anderson describes her and Heap's recent arrest and preliminary hearing on obscenity charges. She then alerts the reader to their upcoming trial, scheduled for the early part of next year. Anderson states,

❝ I know practically everything that will be said in court, both by the prosecution and the defense. I disagree with practically everything that will be said by both. *I do not admit that the issue [of obscenity] is debatable."*

❧ DECEMBER 20, 1920 ❧
WEST 12TH STREET
NEW YORK CITY, NEW YORK

Poet Edna St. Vincent Millay, 28, is writing to her mother, still lingering in the Cape Cod cottage they shared for a time this summer.

Edna St. Vincent Millay

Just last week, Edna had gone to the wedding of her sister Kathleen, 23, here in New York at the Hotel Brevort. Her sister looked uncomfortable; probably because she was regretting giving up a modelling opportunity to marry this guy. Edna had been feeling weak; mostly because of the botched abortion she had a few weeks before.

But Edna just tells her mother that she had bronchitis and been "quite sick… [from] a small nervous breakdown."

The good news is that *Vanity Fair*, where Edna has been having her poems published quite regularly, is going to pay her a good price for the stories she has been selling to rival magazine *Ainslee's* under her pseudonym, Nancy Boyd. *Ainslee's* has offered to double her fee if they could use her real name, but she wants to keep a distance between that popular trash she writes and her more serious poetry.

Better yet, *Vanity Fair* is making her a foreign correspondent and sending her to Paris in the beginning of the new year. She explains to her mother that she desperately needs to get away from New York.

Millay tells one of her beaus, *Vanity Fair* managing editor Edmund "Bunny" Wilson, 25,

❝   I'll be 30 in a minute!"

Edna finishes the letter to her mother and starts packing a trunk for France: Her blue silk umbrella. A pair of velvet galoshes with fur trim. And, of course, her portable Corona typewriter.

❧ CHRISTMAS EVE ❧
DECEMBER 24, 1920
8 RUE DUPUYTREN, LEFT BANK, PARIS

It's been a good year for American ex-patriate bookstore owner Sylvia Beach, 33.

Her shop, Shakespeare & Company, has been open here for more than a year now, despite economic uncertainty in the city. She wrote recently to her sister back in New Jersey:

Valery Larbaud

" My business is maintaining itself in spite of crashes all about. The Bon Marche, the Louvre, the Printemps, different automobile manufacturers and other goods are tottering on the brink. The Galeries [Lafayette] are very low indeed they do say. No one will buy anything till the prices drop and the manufacturers and shops are left with floods of stuff on their hands which they would rather hold on to than sell at a sacrifice—*naturellement*."

She has seen an increase in both the subscribers to her lending library and the other American and British ex-patriates who gather in her shop.

Beach has taken on one particular Irish writer, James Joyce, 38, as a special project. She loved his novel, *A Portrait of the Artist as a Young Man*, and has been supporting him now that he is working on a formidable opus, *Ulysses*.

This year it has been serialized in a "little mag" in New York City, *The Little Review*, but issues have been confiscated by the authorities and the publisher and editor are awaiting trial on obscenity charges!

From talking with Joyce, Sylvia knows that the magazine's lawyer, John Quinn, 50, who buys up pieces of the original manuscript as Joyce writes it, is trying to convince the stubborn Irishman to withdraw his novel from *The Little Review* and have a legitimate American publisher—like Huebsch or Boni and Liveright—bring out a private edition of the whole work when it is finished. This would be treated differently under the law, as it wouldn't be sent through the mail, the way the magazine is.

Joyce is having none of it. He sends cryptic cables to Quinn, written in code, and Quinn telegraphs back, exasperated.

Today, Beach has arranged a special meeting for Joyce.

Sylvia and her partner, Adrienne Monnier, 28, who owns the nearby French language bookshop, La Maison des Amis des Livres, have been trying to introduce Joyce into the literary life of Paris. Today they have invited Valery Larbaud, 39, the posh French poet, who recently gave a talk in Adrienne's store, to meet Joyce. Larbaud was impressed by *Portrait*, which he read on Sylvia's recommendation, and has expressed a desire to meet the author.

Larbaud has many influential friends in the French literary establishment, and Sylvia and Adrienne think the two men will hit it off.

Tomorrow, they are going with Larbaud to an elegant midnight Christmas party with some of their other French friends.

Sylvia has already made her New Year's resolutions which will make 1921 even better: No more coffee, tea or cigarettes. Lots more nights at the Ballets Russes and Comedie Francaise.

❧ DECEMBER 29, 1920 ❧
38 WEST 59TH STREET, CENTRAL PARK SOUTH NEW YORK CITY, NEW YORK

Charles Scribner's Sons' hit novelist, **F. Scott Fitzgerald**, 24, has had a good year, his first as a successful writer.

His income from writing totals $18,850. His first novel, *This Side of Paradise*, is both a financial and critical success, with sales at over 40,000 copies. His follow-up short story collection, *Flappers and Philosophers*, is also doing quite well.

And he married the woman of his dreams, Zelda Sayre, 20. This is as happy as he has been since he was 18.

Now that he has just about finished his second novel, *The Beautiful and Damned*, **Scott** and Zelda are pleased to be out of Westport, Connecticut, where they spent the summer. They are back in Manhattan, in this brownstone near their favorite hotel, The Plaza. The **Fitzgeralds** have dinner sent over from there often. Other nights, they just dine on olive sandwiches and Bushmill's. [Zelda isn't much of a cook.]

However, **Scott's** bank has informed him that they can no longer lend him any money against the security of the stock he holds. He has $6,000 in bills piled up, and he will have to pay back his agent the $600 advance he got for a short story he can't write. **Scott** feels he just can NOT do another flapper.

At the beginning of this month, **Fitzgerald** had written to ask his very understanding Scribner's editor, Max Perkins, 36,

❝   Can this nth advance be arranged?"

Now he is planning to write to Max again to see if he can get a loan as an advance on this second novel. Zelda wants a new squirrel coat.

Farther down Manhattan, in the Scribner's offices, the president, Charles Scribner II, 66, is catching up on his correspondence with an old friend, Sir Shane Leslie, 35, Irish writer and diplomat, who first brought the unpublished **Scott Fitzgerald** to Scribner's attention.

Earlier in the year he had written to Leslie:

❝ Your intro of... **Fitzgerald** proved to be an important one for us;...*Paradise* has been our best seller this season and is still going strong."

Fur coat ad

Today, Scribner writes to Leslie that he does not like the choice of title for **Fitzgerald's** short story collection, *Flappers and Philosophers*, but he's willing go with Perkins' recommendation—the editor has usually been right about these things.

Scribner goes on to say that **Fitzgerald**,

❝ is very fond of the good things of life and is disposed to enjoy it to the full while the going is good. Economy is not one of his virtues."

❧ DECEMBER 31, 1920/ ❧ JANUARY 1, 1921

What a year. **F. Scott Fitzgerald's** predicted "greatest, gaudiest spree in history" hasn't materialized—yet.

At the end of the first year of the new decade...

In Ireland, Irish poet and playwright **William Butler Yeats**, 55, and his wife Georgie, 28, are at home, still resting up after an extensive and successful American lecture tour. They are pleased to be back with their daughter, Anne, almost two, and **Yeats** is continuing to work on his autobiography. He has finally admitted to himself that his father, painter John Butler Yeats, 81, is never going to leave the comfortable life he has in New York City to come back to Ireland.

Parade in Dublin

In England, novelist **Virginia Woolf**, 38, and her husband, **Leonard**, 40, are spending the holidays at their Sussex home, Monk's House near Rodmell. Their almost six-year old project, the Hogarth Press, has lost one of its authors, Katherine Mansfield, 31, to a more established publisher because they had neglected to contract her for more than one book.

And their latest assistant, Ralph Partridge, 26, has only earned £56 as his share of the company yearly profits. But they have printed and published four titles—including **Virginia's** *Kew Gardens*, which has sold 620 copies—and earned 68 pounds, 19 shillings, 4 pence.

The original Hogarth printing press

1920 Ford touring car

In Paris, American ex-patriate writer **Gertrude Stein**, 46, and her partner, **Alice B. Toklas**, 43, have recently welcomed a new member of their household on the Left Bank—Godiva, their new Ford touring car. Their previous auto, "Auntie Pauline," which took them all over France as they volunteered for the Fund for French Wounded during the

Great War, had finally died right in front of the Luxembourg Palace, the 17th century government building. The replacement arrived and **Alice** remarked that it was naked—no clock, no cigarette lighter, no ashtray. So **Gertrude** promptly named her Godiva.

The Algonquin Hotel

In New York, free-lance writer **Dorothy Parker**, 27, is floating. She's getting plenty of her articles and poetry published in magazines, and lunching most days with her fellow writers at the midtown Manhattan Algonquin Hotel. Two of her lunchmates and former *Vanity Fair* colleagues, **Bob Benchley**, 31, and Robert Sherwood, 24, are willing to accept silly pieces she submits to their monthly humor magazine, *Life*, and the *Saturday Evening Post* is willing to buy the same kind of fluff. **Dottie** knows that it is not her best work. But it pays the bills.

What will the new year bring?

TO READ...

Quentin Bell. *Virginia Stephen, 1882-1912*, and *Mrs. Woolf, 1912-1941*. Vols. I and II of his *Virginia Woolf: A Biography*. London: Hogarth Press, 1972. His uncle Leonard Woolf asked him to write it and he did a great job.

A. Scott Berg. *Max Perkins: Editor of Genius*. New York: E. P. Dutton, 1978. The full excellent biography, by the Pulitzer-prize winning *Lindbergh* and Katharine Hepburn biographer.

Kevin Birmingham. *The Most Dangerous Book: The Battle for James Joyce's* Ulysses. New York: The Penguin Press, 2014. Detailed look at the struggle to get *Ulysses* published. God bless Sylvia Beach.

Michael Cunningham. *The Hours*. New York: Farrar, Straus and Giroux, 1998. A well-deserved Pulitzer went to this creative and fascinating novel that, like *Mrs. Dalloway*, weaves three stories in different time periods together. Woolf's original title for her novel was *The Hours*.

Kathleen Dixon Donnelly. *Manager as Muse: Max Perkins' Work with F. Scott Fitzgerald, Ernest Hemingway, and Thomas Wolfe*. Birmingham, UK: K. Donnelly Communications, 2014. 'Nuff said.

Noel Riley Fitch. *Sylvia Beach and the Lost Generation: A History of Literary Paris in the Twenties and Thirties*. New York: W. W. Norton and Co. A detailed and fascinating look at this amazing woman and her friendships with the other characters in Paris at the time.

Brendan Gill. *Here at* The New Yorker. New York: Random House, 1975. The semi-official biography of the magazine up until the 70s.

Arlen J. Hansen. *Expatriate Paris: A Cultural and Literary Guide to Paris of the 1920s*. New York: Arcade Publishing, 2012. In an almanac format organized by areas of the city, this chronicles who was there and where they lived. Good to take with you when you go.

Ernest Hemingway. *A Moveable Feast*. New York: Charles Scribner's Sons, 1964. His version of events, as he remembered them years later.

Marion Meade. *Bobbed Hair and Bathtub Gin: Writers Running Wild in the Twenties, Edna St. Vincent Millay, Dorothy Parker, Zelda Fitzgerald, and Edna Ferber*. New York: Harcourt, Inc., 2004. Meade does well expanding her Parker research to include the other fabulous women.

Marion Meade. *Dorothy Parker: What Fresh Hell Is This?* London: Heinemann, 1988. The best. Excellent biography and the basis for the film, *Mrs. Parker and the Vicious Circle* as well as the A&E *Biography* program.

James R. Mellow. *Charmed Circle: Gertrude Stein and Company*. New York: Avon Books, 1974. The best overall book about this era and the characters in Paris.

Emily Midorikawa and Emma Claire Sweeney. *A Secret Sisterhood*. London: Aurum Press, 2017. A terrific look at the literary friendships of Austen, Bronte, Eliot and Woolf by two great friends of mine in the UK. They also run a fascinating website on female literary friendships, www. SomethingRhymed.wordpress.com.

Ulick O'Connor. *Celtic Dawn: A Portrait of the Irish Literary Renaissance*. London: Black Swan, 1984. The best history of the whole time period and the characters involved.

Diane Souhami. *Gertrude and Alice*. New York: Pandora, 1991. Better than a biography of either one of them, the author writes about both equally and, most interesting, about their relationship.

Frances Spalding. *Vanessa Bell*. London: Weidenfield and Nicolson, 1983. In writing about Roger Fry she discovered Vanessa Bell and wrote this definitive biography. I'm including this one of her books, because it's my favorite. But anything by her is great.

Gertrude Stein. *The Autobiography of Alice B. Toklas*. New York: Vintage Books, 1990. If you've ever been afraid to read Stein, this is the place to start. Definitely her point of view, and a wonderful romp.

Colm Toibin. *Lady Gregory's Toothbrush*. London: Picador, 2003. The title comes from her comment after the *Playboy* riots, "It's the old battle between those who use a toothbrush and those who don't." By the Irish author of the novel *Brooklyn*.

Colm Toibin. *Mad, Bad, Dangerous to Know: The Fathers of Wilde, Yeats and Joyce*. London: Penguin, 2018. Terrific book about three amazing Irishmen—and their sons.

TO WATCH...

Albert Nobbs [2011]. Glenn Close, Janet McTeer. There aren't really any feature films about the Irish Literary Renaissance—and neither is this one. But it is a beautiful evocation of Dublin in the late 19th century. A long time labor of love for Close, it netted her and McTeer Oscar nominations.

Carrington. [1995] Jonathan Pryce, Emma Thompson. Excellent film about the relationship between Lytton Strachey and his partner, Dora Carrington. The beginning scenes show the Bloomsbury group at Vanessa Bell's Sussex house, Charleston, where it was filmed.

Genius. [2016] Colin Firth, Jude Law, Laura Linney. Max Perkins editing a novel doesn't sound like much of a basis for a film, but Firth's Perkins and Law's bombastic Tom Wolfe strike just the right note. Linney as Perkins' wife is the only American actor as a main character, and all filming was done in the UK. Go figure.

The Hours. [2002] Nicole Kidman, Meryl Streep. Award-winning film version of Michael Cunningham's book (see above). The scenes of Los Angeles in the 1950s were all filmed where we lived in Hollywood, Florida.

Midnight in Paris. [2011] Owen Wilson, Kathy Bates. Directed by Woody Allen, who is in love with the city and the time period. "I am Dali!"

Mrs. Dalloway. [1997] Vanessa Redgrave, Rupert Graves, Natascha McElhone. Directed by Marleen Gorris, Redgrave was a great choice to portray Virginia's favorite heroine.

Mrs. Parker and the Vicious Circle. [1994] Jennifer Jason Leigh, Scott Campbell, Matthew Broderick. Excellent film based on Meade's biography of Parker (see above). It has the look and feel of the time and the characters. Yes, she did mumble like that, so you might want to have the rewind button handy. There are numerous clips on YouTube.

Paris Was a Woman [1996]. This terrific documentary focuses on the female relationships in Paris in the 1920s, with a lot about Sylvia Beach's support of James Joyce.

The Ten-Year Lunch. [1987] Good documentary about the whole group, narrated by Heywood Broun's son, CBS sportscaster Heywood Hale Broun. Includes interviews with Marc Connelly, Helen Hayes, Ruth Gordon, and Averell Harriman, among others. A bit outdated, but they're all dead anyway.

TO VISIT...

The Abbey Theatre [https://www.abbeytheatre.ie/]. On Abbey Street in Dublin, the theatre came up with a creative schedule for a COVID19 2020 season, so there is a lot you can experience on line at their site and on Facebook. They also have a very detailed archive of all their productions.

The Algonquin Hotel [https://www.algonquinhotel.com/]. At 59 West 44th Street, the hotel has been refurbished many times and each new owner has pledged to retain its literary history. The latest Algonquin cat, Hamlet, has his own Facebook page, but hasn't been very active lately.

BloggingWoolf [https://bloggingwoolf.wordpress.com/]. Run by Paula Maggio of Kent State University, this is one of the best blogs to follow for all things Woolfian.

Charleston. [https://www.charleston.org.uk/]. On your next European trip— Go. You'll have to drive or take a taxi from nearby Lewes, but it is well worth it, particularly during their May festival.

Coole Park. [https://www.coolepark.ie/]. Lady Gregory's home about 35km south of Galway city, near Gort, is now a national park, without the house but with the autograph tree. Well worth a visit next time you are driving around the west of Ireland.

The Dorothy Parker Society [https://www.facebook.com/groups/dorothyparkersociety]. This Facebook group is run by Kevin Fitzpatrick and you can find all of his terrific books there. When you're planning to go to New York again, check out his walking tours. For 20 years he has been keeping the flame with events and publications. Highly recommended.

The Dublin Literary Pub Crawl [https://www.dublinpubcrawl.com/]. My main Dublin tip, particularly for your first night there. Two actors lead a group of tourists around the main part of the city, stopping to do scenes from Irish literature and theatre, punctuated by drinks in pubs. Great way to get the lay of the land. Until the COVID 19 shutdown is over, you can buy their book from the site.

Monk's House [https://www.nationaltrust.org.uk/monks-house]. Virginia and Leonard's country home is part of the National Trust, well worth a visit, and not far from Charleston.

The National Library of Ireland [www.nli.ie]. The Library has the best exhibit about Yeats and all his "Such Friends," and I've seen a lot of them. You can access it online and, eventually, in person. Great gift shop—and, ladies, use the downstairs restroom. Trust me.

Shakespeare & Co. [https://www.facebook.com/groups/131979076789] Until we can travel again, you can join their Facebook group. The real shop is on a totally different site, directly across from Notre Dame, but worth a visit. Then go sit in one of the cafes. They are still there.

Sissinghurst. [https://www.nationaltrust.org.uk/sissinghurst-castle-garden] Vita Sackville-West's home is known especially for its gorgeous gardens. If you can, stay at the B&B on the grounds.

"Such Friends" [Suchfriends.wordpress.com]. On the blog I am currently chronicling The Literary 1920s. Hopefully, there will be nine more books.

"Such Friends": The Founding of the Abbey Theatre, and Dorothy Parker and the Algonquin Round Table [http://www.picttheatre.org/pict-educates/]. The webinars that I did for PICT Classical Theatre are available to replay for free. On the same site there are also two talks about John Millington Synge.

"Such Friends": Virginia Woolf and the Bloomsbury Group [www.voicemap. me]. My own walking tour of the area is available to download for your mobile or computer.

"Thoor Ballylee" [https://yeatsthoorballylee.org/home/], Yeats' tower, "with the river on the first floor," as Ezra Pound said, is near Coole Park, and also worth the trip when it is open again. They often sponsor events in the summer around his June birthday.

ABOUT THE AUTHOR

Kathleen Dixon Donnelly, Ph. D.

Kathleen Dixon Donnelly has been involved in teaching and the creative process for more than 40 years. Her thesis for her MBA from Duquesne University in her hometown of Pittsburgh, Pennsylvania, was *Manager as Muse: Maxwell Perkins' Work with F. Scott Fitzgerald, Ernest Hemingway and Thomas Wolfe,* available on Amazon in both print and Kindle versions.

"Such Friends": The Literary 1920s is based in part on her dissertation for her Ph.D. in Communications from Dublin City University, on the creative development of writers in early 20th century salons.

She has led walking and driving tours of Dublin and Coole Park in Ireland; London and Sussex in England; and the Left Bank of Paris. You can walk with her through Bloomsbury by downloading her tour, *"Such Friends": Virginia Woolf and the Bloomsbury Group* from www.voicemap.me. She has given numerous presentations about the writers throughout the United Kingdom at the Southbank Centre, the University of the Third Age, and in the United States at the English Speaking Union, and Osher Lifelong Learning programs.

Kathleen has self-published a series of books from her blogs as *Gypsy Teacher,* chronicling her voyages on Semester at Sea and relocation to the United Kingdom, available on Amazon.

She recently retired as a senior lecturer in both the School of Media and Business School at Birmingham [UK] City University. She lives with her Irish husband Tony Dixon and their cat, Willie Yeats, in Pittsburgh.

You can contact her by email at kaydee@gypsyteacher.com, through Twitter @SuchFriends, or through her blog, www.suchfriends.wordpress.com.